Enjoy Success Today

How to Start and Build a Thriving Business... and Still Have a Life!

Jared James

BookLocker.com, Inc.
2009

Editor: Deirdre Silberstein of Silberstein & Associates LLC
Book Cover and Interior Design: Meg Russell Rideout of MR2Designs
Cover Photography: Rick Olszewski of Rick O Photography

Acknowledgments

A lot has gone into writing this book, but I want to thank the many people who have had a part in shaping me over the years. First and foremost, to my mother, for raising me and instilling so many of the traits in me that I have put into action to get to where I am. To my father: Thanks for being a good friend and always encouraging me to pursue my dreams. Whenever I have come to you with a thought or a vision, I could always count on you to encourage me to move forward.

To my pastor, Bishop Jay Ramirez: Thanks for taking me under your wing ever since I was a young kid and seeing something different in me. I have always been able to count on you as a sounding board in anything I was doing, to have you consider different angles I may not have seen, and to trust that you would tell me exactly what you thought.

To my two boys, Grayson and Noah: You are both too young to read this yet, but you both provide me with so much motivation to keep growing and changing. I hope one day you will both pick this book up, and it will help you guys find success for yourselves.

Lastly, to my wife: We have been together for almost half of my life and I can't fathom life without you. You definitely will tell me what others won't, and that is invaluable. I thank God that I have you and that I am lucky enough to be married to someone who still makes me want to leave the office every day and come home. Our kids are so blessed to have you as a mother, and I am blessed to share my life with you. I love you always.

— Jared James

Disclaimer

This book details the author's personal experiences with and opinions about personal and professional success. The author is not a professional services provider.

The author and publisher are providing this book and its contents on an "as is" basis and make no representations or warranties of any kind with respect to this book or its contents. The author and publisher disclaim all such representations and warranties, including for example warranties of merchantability and success for a particular purpose. In addition, the author and publisher do not represent or warrant that the information accessible via this book is accurate, complete or current.

Except as specifically stated in this book, neither the author or publisher, nor any authors, contributors, or other representatives will be liable for damages arising out of or in connection with the use of this book. This is a comprehensive limitation of liability that applies to all damages of any kind, including (without limitation) compensatory; direct, indirect or consequential damages; loss of data, income or profit; loss of or damage to property and claims of third parties.

You understand that this book is not intended as a substitute for consultation with a licensed legal, financial or other professional provider, such as your attorney, financial advisor, or certified public accountant.

This book provides content related to personal and professional success. As such, use of this book implies your acceptance of this disclaimer.

Table of Contents

Introduction

It is not uncommon for someone to stop me and ask, "To what do you attribute your success" or "What are you doing differently?" If I have a lot to do or am short on time, I will simply answer by saying that I guess I am just lucky. The truth is, I don't really believe that one person is luckier than another. I believe that people create their own luck or, more accurately, when opportunities come their way some people are better prepared for them and are better able to convert them into success. Other people have plenty of opportunities, but it is what people do with their opportunities and how well they are prepared for them that really matters. That, in a nutshell, is what this book will be about. I will answer the question, "What do you do differently?" once and for all.

Why do people ask me about my success? Because, before I turned 27, I ran one of the top two real estate teams in the state of Connecticut and built a real estate business that did over $30,000,000 in sales volume. I also run a company called Jared James Enterprises and travel around the country speaking to Realtors and showing them how to be successful in any economic climate. I have even been honored by *Realtor Magazine* in their annual 30 under 30 issue, which highlights 30 people in real estate in America under the age of 30.

If you are taking the time to read this book, you are already light years ahead of your peers. You would be amazed at how many people become parents and never read about parenting or go on vacation and never research their destinations. The same principle applies to being in business. I have always thought that a lot of my success happened so quickly because, in my head, I was already there. I mean that, while in the beginning I didn't have any experience negotiating or making tough decisions, I had read about many successful people doing so, and I played out their actions and analyzed their decisions in my head to see what I would have done. When I was facing similar situations in real life, I felt like an old pro.

Over the years, many people have told me they were surprised by my age when they met me in person after doing business with me over the phone. They expected someone older. I attribute this to my business approach. I never acted like a rookie because I didn't feel like a rookie. My rookie years were played in the stadium of my own head, something I would recommend to all readers of this book. Learn to play things out in your head accurately. To do this, you have to understand personalities and human nature. You have to develop your skills and perceptions. But most importantly, you have to understand yourself (a whole other book altogether).

In the beginning, I really struggled with the idea of writing a book on the topic of success. There are so many books available already, so I wondered "What's the point?" Then I realized that my book would be written by someone who has already had great career success, but who does not fit the profile of the white-haired, mid-50s, male author. I respect those authors, and I'll be one of them one day, but that is not my story now. All of the successes and failures I'll write about in this book happened before the age of 30.

I want to help others understand how I achieved my success and how they, too, can be successful. In Part One of this book, I'll talk about how to start building your future now, in both your business and personal lives. I can remember being a student and being more interested in getting ahead than in partying. While others were still wondering what to do with their lives, I was planning the next steps in my own life. When you realize that the people around you all want to be successful, but rarely do what is required, you will realize that by simply doing what is required to be successful you will separate yourself from the pack. Being successful does not require a genius-level IQ or a Harvard MBA. These can help, but with the right mindset, attitude, training, and skill set, just about anyone can achieve success.

If you go too far one way or the other, whether toward business or personal, your life will be out of balance and will ultimately contradict the idea of success.

One of the important points I always try to drive home is that business and personal success are not separate matters. Projecting one means projecting the other and creating balance in your whole life. I'll use the word 'balance' throughout this book. If you go too far one way or the other, whether toward business or personal, your life will be out of balance and will ultimately contradict the idea of success. My business successes mean nothing to me if I do not enjoy going home and sharing my successes with my family. My personal successes are limited if I have a constant feeling of anxiety about how to provide for the people that I love so much.

Success starts when people accurately assess where they are in their lives, recognize what their strengths and weaknesses are, figure out what they love to do, and then take this assessment and turn it into a successful lifestyle. I know that everyone has a role in life, a purpose. Some are called to be leaders and some are called to be followers. Without the followers, there would be no leaders, because there'd be no one to lead if no one is following. This same principle applies to business. Some are great entrepreneurs and are called to work for themselves; others are great associates and find their role in working for someone else's business. Figuring out what you are will save you a lot of stress, and most importantly in my mind, it will save you a lot of time.

In Part Two, I talk about the skills and attitudes needed for success. There is no doubt that having passion can get you somewhere, but only so far. At some point, you have to develop the skills needed not only to compete with your competition, but win against your competition. The only way you can achieve this is to be the best prepared and most knowledgeable person in your field. You can never stop learning and must always want to grow as a whole person. Some entrepreneurs focus solely on their inner selves – their attitudes, mindsets, and spirituality. Others focus solely on their outer selves – their appearance, skill sets, and knowledge base. To win, you have to continually build both your inner and outer selves. You cannot ignore one or the other and expect to achieve success.

Even when I was in school, I can remember thinking about the strategies and personality types that tended to be more successful than others. I thought about the concept of speed of implementation and what that means. I also realized that, if you're always doing what everyone else is doing, you will only get to where they get to. The follow-the-herd mentality will only get you to where the herd goes. If you are going to follow anyone, follow those who have achieved great things. Think about it. When was the last time you read the biography of someone named Average Joe? We are not drawn to people that have achieved the ordinary. We are drawn to people who have achieved the extraordinary, and that is the way it should be.

Time is your most valuable resource you have. It doesn't fluctuate like money. It doesn't have bad moods and good moods like people. It is the same everyday regardless of the day. It is also the most commonly mismanaged resource or asset. Time can be your best friend or your worst enemy, but in the end it is yours to use either way. It doesn't surprise you or sneak up on you, unless you're not managing it well. I will write a whole chapter on this topic because I think it is that important.

Efficiency is another key to success. My career has been built on finding ways to work smarter than everyone else around me. If you can find a way to not only work harder but also smarter, you will fly by those around you.

You will find that, as you become more and more successful, your business will evolve and branch out into new areas. As I am writing this book, I am also recording a series of instructional courses for Realtors to help them achieve success quickly, regardless of the economic climate. Creating these courses is part of another idea I believe in so strongly: developing multiple streams of income from similar businesses so you can concentrate on one overall business every day and not feel as if you are trying to run three different businesses. The key here, as elsewhere, is balance. You will probably find the chapter on developing multiple streams of income to be one of your favorites, because it will challenge you to think of new ways to create additional income. I think we can agree that having more income is never a bad thing.

This will be a great book for young people, college students, or recent graduates wondering how to become a success quickly. This will also be a great book for people who have had some level of success in business and in life, but have never been able to take it to the next level. This book will not reveal shortcuts, but rather the attitudes, practices, and skills that will get you further.

If you are a young person reading this book, I hope that you will be inspired by my story and apply the principles in the coming pages to create your own success. It is important for you to understand that you don't look the part of success and, in many cases, don't act the part of success, either. The good news is that both your look and actions are under your control. There is no doubt that an older person has a distinct advantage over a young person. When an older, more mature person walks into a room for negotiations, it is assumed that he or she is credible until proven otherwise. That is not the case when you are younger.

Fortunately, knowledge and wisdom can both be attained at any age, if you want them enough. Knowledge is easier to gain, because it really just requires the time and dedication needed to learn. Wisdom is different. Wisdom isn't gained by simply reading so many pages or watching the History Channel. Wisdom is gained on the inside. If you want to gain wisdom, observe and study how wise people make their decisions. You have to train how you process information, almost like a math equation, and understand that your thought processes can be influenced for the positive, as well as for the negative. At a certain point, acting wisely becomes second nature to you. If you want to attain just one trait, become wise, now; don't wait until you are older. Wisdom is also gained through humility. I like the way John Wooded put it: "It is what you learn after you know it all."

If you are reading this book and you do not believe that you are still in your youthful days, be encouraged, because you, too, can use the principles I did to attain success. You are also fortunate enough not to have to deal with the obstacles that youth can bring.

My whole career has been focused on getting to where I want to be in the most efficient manner, while still building a solid foundation. The foundation of your life and of your business can no more be ignored than the foundation of your house. This book may also be for people who never built that foundation, people who have grown too quickly or who have business or personal lives that looks great on the outside, but may be about to crumble. Sometimes, you have to be willing to tear everything down and start over in the right way, instead of constantly patching every hole, fixing every door knob, and carpeting over every uneven floor. This book will show how to build your foundation, create your future, and become truly successful in business and in life.

Part I

Building Your Future in Business and Life

Chapter 1

What Do You Want from Life?

What's Your End Game?

It is pointless to spin your wheels trying to succeed if you don't have an end game, that is, you don't know what you are working towards. There has to be a reason why you're working so hard and putting in the sweat and tears. If you don't know what that reason is, you are like a hamster running on the wheel, exerting so much energy only to find out that when you are done, you are exactly where you started, just a little more exhausted. I sometimes picture it as being like a greyhound in a race where they dangle the rabbit just far enough in front of the dogs so they will run with everything they have only to find out they won't get the rabbit and that the whole purpose was someone else's enjoyment.

Obviously, that is an extreme example, but it makes the point. If you don't know what you want from life, you will always be running in place, staying stagnant, or chasing someone else's rabbit for their enjoyment. If you don't have your own goals, someone else will create them for you for their own benefit. Before you can put into practice the principles I am going to lay out in this book, you first have to understand what the point of those principles is. It is not enough to say you want to be successful. *Why* do you want to be successful? It is not enough to say that you want to build something special or create something from nothing. *Why* do you want to do these things?

You will notice that I tend to pose a lot of questions for you to think about. I do this because, if you don't ask yourself these questions, someone else will, and you better know the answers, if you want to have any chance at success.

I always get a kick out of goal-setting meetings. They always focus on the 'what' of the goal and not the 'why.' Without the why, you will lack the true incentive or motivation to achieve your goals. For example, when you set a goal to make $200,000 in a given year without having a purpose for the goal, it is easy to take your foot off the pedal when you get close toward the end of the year and see that the goal will not be reached. But when you want to make $200,000 so you can give away $20,000 so that a single mother with three kids can buy a crib for her newborn and not have to worry about putting food on the table, you have true motivation. You have really gotten to the why of the goal and not just the what. Both are equally important in the goal-setting process.

At a company I worked for in college, they always used to have us write out our goals in three ways. We had our 'must do' goals, which were goals we could meet easily, no matter what happened. Everything could go wrong, and these goals would still be fairly easy to reach. The next were the 'should do' goals, which, if we worked hard and everything went as planned, we should be able to reach. The last were the 'could do' goals, which, if everything went right and the stars were aligned, we could shoot for, but wouldn't get discouraged if we couldn't reach them. This whole process of goal setting was focused on the 'what' of the goals, and all results were number driven. I look back now and think that I was fortunate enough to learn from this process how important goals are and how important it is to write your goals down. But, I always felt that there was a better way to set goals, and there had to be a better way to increase motivation besides thinking about how much money you were going to make for yourself and the company. *Goals should ultimately affect more people than just yourself.*

This brings up the greater point about goals: Not all goals should be so 'you' focused. It is important to see beyond yourself and what you will gain. As I stated earlier, it is much easier to let yourself down and be content with what you almost achieved than it is to picture a newborn not getting a comfortable crib because you didn't get to where you wanted to get to. I tend to use extreme examples like this because sometimes they are what you need to truly motivate yourself. You have to focus on the actual situation at hand and what is at stake to reach your full potential.

Keeping the 'Why' in Mind

The difference between a gold medal winner at the Olympic Games and someone breaking the world record at the Olympic Games is that an athlete may let up at the end of a race because he has it in the bag or has achieved so much. The world record holder, however, understands that he is not just racing against the guys lined up against him. He is racing against history, not just against his competitors. Winning the race would not be enough, because his true goal was to set the world record. History doesn't remember gold medal winners as much as it remembers world records that stand the test of time.

   The perfect example of this is Michael Phelps, a swimmer on the 2008 US Olympic team. Phelps had set out to be the first athlete in history to take home eight gold medals in one Olympics, or so everyone thought. In Phelps' head, he had different goals. The gold medals would only be the results of his pursuing his true goals. In one of his races, his goggles began to fill up with water and he was unable to see where he was going or where his competitors were. He said afterwards that he wasn't even sure if he was going to be able to stay straight in his lane or if he was going to get disqualified for going into someone else's lane because he just couldn't see. He didn't even know how far away he was from the finish line and tried to count his strokes, so he could guess how far away he was and finish strong. In the end, he won the race and set a world record, as well. You would have thought that he would have been overjoyed by this and jumping up and down in the water. To everyone's surprise, he looked rather somber in the water, and nobody could figure out why. It wasn't until afterwards that it was revealed that he was extremely disappointed. Although he had won the gold medal and set the new world record, he hadn't swum the race as quickly as he knew he could have and, therefore, didn't reach the true goal that he had set for himself.

   There are many lessons to take from this example. First, don't let anybody else set goals for you. While everyone was cheering, Phelps knew that he had not done what he set out to do. If he had listened to everyone else and let the whole world pat him on his back, would he have gone on to win the eight gold medals? He has said publicly that not going as fast as he knew he could in that race made him want to get the eight gold medals even more to prove to himself that he was the swimmer that he knew he was.

The same principle works the other way as well. Just as you don't want someone to limit you by setting goals for you, you also don't want someone to always set your goals so high that they are unattainable and you are constantly feeling like a failure because you never reach them. No one knows your abilities and your persona like you do. It is true that many times we need people to push us, but there is a difference between being pushed toward our potential by those who love us and never living up to someone's expectations for us because their expectations are unrealistic. Make sure you know the difference, and if someone is pushing you for the wrong reasons, you need to put an end to that now and start setting realistic goals for yourself.

It is extremely difficult to reach your potential if you don't experience small successes along the way. This is what the 'must do' goal setting got right. When you are constantly reaching for the unattainable – the 'could do' goals – you can get so close so many times and have a lot of the small successes, but always feel like a failure. No one wants this to happen when setting and writing down their goals.

The second lesson from Phelps' experience is to not make excuses. It would have been easy for him to take all of the pressure off of himself by simply stopping and saying that he couldn't see anything and his eyes hurt. Everyone would have understood. How can we expect him to swim if he can't see? He didn't do that, though. He kept going and was determined to achieve his goals.

This brings us to a third lesson we can learn from this race. Sometimes you have to improvise. When the water filled his goggles and blinded him, he simply went back to the basics and started to count the strokes it usually took him to get to the finish line in the pool. One of the major hurdles that many successful people have to overcome is thinking that they can use some complicated equation or problem-solving technique to fix the curveballs life throws at them. If we look at the Michael Phelps, though, we can see that he just went back to the basics, to what he had been doing since he was a little child practicing in the pool.

Learning to improvise to reach your goals works in all aspects of life. I remember the night when I was trying to get my two-year-old son to eat his dinner. On this particular night, my son decided that he did not want to cooperate and was not going to eat. Not only was he not going to eat, but he was going to push away everything we put in front of him and scream whenever we did it. I knew that time was limited, and if I didn't come up with something quickly, he was going to 'lose it' completely. I decided to look at his motives and understand his personality, so I took his plate and made it mine. His plate was set up in front of me and I was now using his fork to pretend I was eating his food. Anyone who has a two-year-old knows that the child may not be in the mood for his own food, but can never resist eating your food. Once my son thought that I was giving him forks full of pork from MY plate, he couldn't eat it fast enough. This just proves that even in my personal life, it was possible to meet one goal by thinking on my feet and improvising.

Recently, I was working with another top realtor on a deal, and we were jockeying for position, trying to make sure that our own client got the better deal than the other side. This other realtor ('Jane Doe') kept making remarks to me that were intended to put me – the younger realtor – in my place and ultimately get what she wanted for her client. I remember thinking that I make twice as much as Jane; I run one of the top two teams in the whole state of Connecticut; I am about to be inducted into the Re/Max Hall of Fame, and so on. I was trying to come up with clever ways to put Jane in her place and let her know what I had accomplished in such a short amount of time. But then a thought came to my mind: "You didn't get to where you are today because you are a prized champion in the art of the peeing contest." I know that sounds strange, but that is exactly how it came out in my head. Then I started to think of what got me to where I am. How did I win such people over at the beginning of my career before I had the 'Impressive Resume?' I took a step back and remembered that the success of my business and of the clients I represented relied heavily on the relationships I had formed and the reputation I had won with the realtors in the area. Instead of arguing back and forth with Jane, I took the diplomatic approach and reminded her in a nice way that we both wanted the same thing. We both had the same objective: We wanted the deal to close. If it didn't close, neither one of us would have won. I apologized for being arrogant and asked her if we could start over. I didn't require any apology from her because it wasn't about that. Ultimately, it was about reaching the goal that I had set for this particular meeting and client.

It was amazing how the whole tone of our conversation shifted. Ten minutes earlier, we had been doing battle on the beaches of Normandy, and now we were working together and trying to find ways to help each other close this deal. The lesson learned here is that I could have used some fancy line I learned at a conference or pulled rank on her based on my production in the business. But by simply humbling myself, I showed her a side of me that she wasn't expecting, and in a sense, threw her a curveball, to which she responded very nicely.

I don't want to devalue the idea of educating yourself and practicing many different problem-solving techniques. Many times, they are necessary and work very well in various situations. I just don't want you to constantly lean on them as a crutch. I was never a big fan of all of the scripted responses I was taught in training courses and books. I understand why they are valuable to many people, but I have always felt that in some circumstances they can do more harm than good. If someone brings up a legitimate issue and I come back with some robotic response, I risk devaluing my relationship with that person, because I have proven to them that I have not truly listened to them at all. All I was doing was calculating a response to their concern, so I wouldn't look as if I didn't know the answer; instead of really hearing them and trying to figure out the solution for this particular situation. The key here is to understand people. You can learn people skills by watching people and how they react. When you are standing in line to get a coffee, watch the people around you. Watch how they interact in conversations with others. Watch how they react if their coffee is not done the right way. You serve yourself and the people around you well by developing this skill. If you are going to be an expert on anything, be an expert on people. This will help you in any business or personal setting that you find yourself in.

Remember Balance When Setting Your Goals

When setting your goals for your life, you need to understand that your life encompasses more than just your business. Whenever I am sitting down to write out my goals for the year or even for the long term, I always have my family in mind. Before I had a family, I would still picture what my family would be like. I knew what cars we would drive, what our neighborhood would look like. I even tried to picture what the atmosphere of my future house would be like. This may sound a little too detailed and even strange to some, but everything you do in your business life affects these personal things too.

For example, I knew that I wanted my wife to experience true happiness, and I didn't want my kids worrying about the things I worried about as a kid. I wanted them to be carefree, not thinking about whether the marshal or landlord was coming to kick them out of their place of security - their home. For this to happen, I knew that I needed to make a certain amount of money, I had to live within my means, and I had to have a certain amount of time to spend with them so they could experience a full relationship with their father. Once I understood this, I understood that there were certain career paths that I could pursue and others that were not going to fit the lifestyle I wanted.

This goes back to the concept of understanding the why of your goals and not just the what. I am a little more focused on my goals at work when I have my children in mind. I want so badly to keep my family in the neighborhood that I had pictured and to allow my wife to live a comfortable life that I am willing to do whatever it takes to make that happen.

If you are making your goals without considering your family life, you may need to rethink your goals. As I said before, your business successes mean nothing without people in your life to share your successes with you. Someday these things will matter to you, and you realize pretty quickly that you only get one life and you do want to make the most of it. Working your life away will leave you empty and wondering in the end "What did I work so hard for?" If you are twenty years old or sixty years old, it is not too late to stop this pattern and start doing things differently. I truly believe that one of the keys to my success at such a relatively young age is my ability to recognize these types of life principles. You won't hear them taught at the majority of success seminars you attend, but they are just as important, if not more important, than any other lesson you learn.

Understanding Your Motivation

When you are setting your goals you have to understand what motivates you. At this point in my life, I am heavily motivated by my love for my family. I won't lie and tell you that I was not heavily motivated by money early on or that I do not still enjoy the sight of a large check. But I've learned: It is not money that motivates me, but the security that money can bring when managed properly. I think many of you can understand what I am saying.

I came from circumstances that many people can relate to. I was not born with a silver spoon in my mouth and did not know what it was like to have a lot of new things while I was growing up. My clothes were usually from a garage sale or were hand-me downs from my older brother. My ability to make a pair of pants, a shirt, or a pair of socks, or any other article of clothing last through the worst disasters comes from this upbringing. I consider this a strength of mine, but my wife would probably disagree. If you think about it, why would you throw out an undershirt with a rip in it? An undershirt's sole purpose is to fit under another shirt, never to be seen, so what does it matter?

I can remember moving many times and living in six different states as a child, which made me a bit insecure. I can remember not telling my mother about a field trip coming up at school, because I didn't want my mother to feel badly if she didn't have the money for it. Over and over again, I was faced with situations that made me feel beneath the other children, because I didn't have what they had. I felt like I had to act a certain way, so I wouldn't blow my cover and let them know that I really didn't enjoy so many of the luxuries that many of them considered normal. Ultimately, these experiences helped to shape me into who I have become and am continuing to become today.

Recently, my son got a toy that required assembly. I have gotten much better at assembling toys, but many people still find humor in what was once my inability to put things together. One particular person asked me who had put my toys together when I was a kid, and my response was that many of my toys came from garage sales, already assembled.

My point in mentioning this is to show you where my motivation for security and my respect for money come from.

In a way, it is like meeting people from the Depression Era who became professional savers. It is not that they attended the best budgeting courses in the world. It is just that certain experiences in your life shape who you become and why you do certain things. Understanding what those experiences are and who you have become as a result is a huge factor in coming up with your goals. In other words, you may not want to pursue your dream of becoming a full-time flight attendant if you were in a plane crash as a child and are deathly afraid of getting on a plane. There is a better way to spend your time – getting an education for a different career and setting different career goals.

Every book on goal setting tells you that you have to write your goals down. I agree, but I believe in taking it one step further and posting your goals in places where you will regularly see them. You can put them up on the mirror in the bathroom or on your refrigerator. It is important that you are constantly reminded about what you are trying to accomplish from the time you wake up until you lay your head down at night. If you are anything like me, you may even ponder them at night while laying in bed. This is not a bad idea, if you are doing it is to strategize how you are going to get where you want to get to or if you are reviewing what you have already done and pondering whether there is a better way to do it next time.

But be careful about sharing your goals with many people. There are short-term goals for losing weight or landing a certain large account for your business, which probably sound attainable to everyone. If your long-term goals have been set correctly, however, not everyone should think they are entirely

---

Enjoy Success Today — 23

reachable. This goes back to the concept that you only have one life to live. Why waste your lifetime with small, very achievable goals?

Your long-term goals should make you stretch. They should make you a little uncomfortable. At times, you should feel discouraged, as if you have set your mark too high. This is the only way that you will achieve the most with what God has given you. The reason people statistically are able to reach higher goals when they have a coach pushing them is that there is something within each one of us that will shut down and give up at a certain point. We are not always able to see the full picture, as someone else can. When setting your long-term goals, reach further than you thought was possible, and you will get further than you thought was possible, even if you don't hit the quantitative measure you were reaching for. It is the old adage that if you reach for nothing, you are sure to get it. Don't be afraid to fail. Failure is part of success and only makes success that more enjoyable. How much more do you appreciate hitting your optimum weight when you know you have struggled over the years to lose weight and have come up short time and time again? The greatest hockey player of all time, Wayne Gretzky, made the statement that you miss 100% of the shots you don't take. I couldn't agree more.

If you are reading this and wondering if what you are currently doing is big enough, then it is possible that it is not. It is also possible that you are doing exactly what you are supposed to do. We live in a culture that values certain things

> *Failure is part of success and only makes success that more enjoyable.*

and devalues others. One of the greatest callings you can have is to raise children. This goes back to knowing who you are. Some people are supposed to be great nurses and doctors. Not everyone is called to run their own business, as I am. Finding out where you belong will save you a lot of time, heartache, and disappointment. Being positioned where you belong is better than making millions of dollars, only to realize years down the line that you hate what you do and what you really should have been doing with your life over the years was being a teacher.

Life is full of surprises and will probably not go exactly as you plan. But I guarantee you: If you think in great detail about the things I have laid out and plan in great detail how you want to get there, your life will not stray far from the picture that you dreamed of in your head. I am living proof of this. It does not have to take fifty years to accomplish. Although it is a lifelong journey, you should begin to see the fruit of your labor very quickly. I didn't get to where I am in such a short amount of time because I waited for things to happen. At some point, you *must* take action and make things happen. If you sit on the sidelines waiting, you will become a part of the crowd. I would rather be a player on the field every day of the week. Think of yourself in reference to the news. There are those who watch the news, those who report the news, and those who make the news. Which do you want to be? Your answer to that question will go a long way in determining where you fit in. While reading this book, the question of what you want from life is going to come up over and over again. I hope by the time you finish reading, you will be able to answer that very important question.

Chapter 2

Where Are You Now?

I was talking with a friend recently about this book, and he mentioned a very important point: He has read every single book on the market about getting to the next level or being successful, but none of them helped him get from where he was currently to where he could really start to apply the lessons that those books taught. Sometimes, it's as if there is a ladder in front of you that reaches high into the clouds and, if you climb it, it brings you to greater levels of success and fulfillment in your life and business than you ever dreamed possible. The problem is that you are not even at a place where you can reach the ladder and start to climb. You are standing five feet away, stuck in quicksand, and you just can't get to the ladder, no matter how hard you try.

The truth is that, unless you understand where you are now, you can't start to apply the lessons from books that want to help you succeed. This doesn't apply just to people who are struggling. It also applies to people who are at various levels of success. You should never feel comfortable staying where you are for a long period of time. Stagnancy leads to death, or at minimum decay. It is like a house that becomes vacant, and the air stops circulating, mold starts to form, and the bugs and animals start to take over. Regardless of where you are now, you should not only welcome and adapt to change, you should ultimately become an innovator of change.

One of my favorite stories in the Bible is in Genesis, right after Adam disobeyed God. Adam is hiding, and the story tells us that God goes through the Garden simply asking, "Adam, where are you?" Many people wonder why God didn't know where Adam was. The answer is simple: God wasn't asking Adam where he was as if he was playing hide-and-seek. God was asking, "Where are you?" because he wanted Adam to realize for himself where he was. Sometimes, it is better for us to realize for ourselves where we are instead of having someone else tell us.

I tell this story, because I know that there is a tendency to read a book like this one and to want to go out and do everything at once. After all, the key to success is the speed at which you implement the new ideas that you gain. But before you can start to do this with the hope of any real success, you have to take a moment and figure out where you are right now. Not tomorrow, not yesterday, but right now.

You should never feel comfortable staying where you are for a long period of time.

I have told you a little bit about my upbringing and how fortunate I was to have a childhood that taught me to not expect to have things handed to me. I knew a lot of great people, but I didn't see too many of them really achieve a whole lot of material success. My mother worked very hard, did a great job of raising three boys, and set a great example for me and my brothers in many ways, but I never really had a model of an all- encompassing successful life.

As I got older, I realized that not having that model could be very positive for me, because I knew enough to recognize that I needed to find models to help me shape my life and my decisions. This is where many people make a mistake. They either deny that they need someone to look up to or they look up to the wrong people. I promise you this: Everyone is following someone. Without something or somebody to look up to, you are like an arrow without a target. If you never aim for something, you are sure not to hit it. You will just wander around day-to-day like a sleepwalker, without any real passion, drive, or aspirations. You will grow up, go to college if you are lucky, get a job, get married, have kids, and proceed through life without any real purpose or passion. Then you will wonder, is this what life is really all about? I would hope not.

There are four distinct areas of life – relationships, emotional status, decision-making ability, finances – about which you need to ask the question, "Where am I?"

Relationships

People mean many things when they talk about relationships. The first thing I think of is my relationship with God, but I am going to cover that topic in another chapter. Almost as important, though, are your relationships with other people and with yourself.

With Other People

In today's difficult economy, there are great opportunities for starting your own business and going to work for yourself. Some of the wealthiest men and women of all time started creating their fortunes during the Great Depression. This happened for two reasons: (1) many people lost their jobs and had to start their own businesses because they had no other choice; and (2) the greatest business minds find ways not only to survive, but to grow in tough times; while everyone else is downsizing or going out of business, they are finding ways to work smarter and grow their market share. Great minds find a need and fill it. It is that simple.

Even so, regardless of their field, all businesspeople depend on their relationships with others. When I got into real estate, the first thing I did was have lunch with some of the people that I thought could help me. I told them what I was doing, explained how I could help them, and outlined how I expected them to help me. Without these relationships, I would have been starting below ground-level, trying to claw my way to the top. But because of these relationships, the day I announced my intentions, I had three or four 'walking billboards' ready to tell everyone what I did and why they should use me. It didn't matter that I hadn't done a deal in my life. It didn't matter that I didn't know many other realtors or mortgage brokers. It didn't matter that I had a client list and a database of zero. All that mattered was that these people knew me, they had a relationship with me, and they trusted me enough to send their clients to me. Nothing is more powerful in business than a personal referral.

If you are thinking of starting a business or want to grow yours, one of the first things you have to analyze is the strength of your relationships with other people. Do you have a lot of conflicts? Do people trust you? Do people like to be around you? Do people tend to ask you questions in social gatherings, or are you the one asking the questions and getting "Yes" or

"No" answers? You have to ask yourself these questions and answer them honestly.

The good news is that if you don't like the answers to these questions, you still have time to fix things. Usually there is something that you are doing or something about the way you act or behave that drives people to feel a certain way about you. Pick three people that you consider close and trustworthy, and ask them their opinion of you. This is not a time to become offended or defend yourself. This must be done confidentially to help you better your character.

This may sound like a strange thing to do, but believe it or not, I did it about seven or eight years ago. It wasn't easy, but it was productive. I went to someone I really trusted, who I knew thought a lot of me, but who I also knew would be honest without being malicious. I took what that person said to heart and am eternally grateful. I truly believe that if I had not made the changes that I needed to, I would not be where I am today.

> *There is nothing worse than having someone constantly tell you that you are not going to be anything and that your dreams are crazy.*

Another reason why relationships are so important is that others have power over you. You have to be careful not to give people power casually, but anyone who is married knows that you do not function at your best when you are at odds with your spouse. Men especially like to act as if they don't care, and I have been guilty of this on more than one occasion. If you truly love your spouse, though, you will be affected if the two of you are not acting and feeling as one. You can play over and over in your head why you are right and why he or she needs to see that. The bottom line, though, is that if you want to perform at your peak ability, you need to get this relationship back on course. There is nothing worse than having someone constantly tell you that you are not going to be anything and that your dreams are crazy. Thank God, I don't have this at home, but I have seen it. I have seen people's whole businesses destroyed due to a bad marriage relationship. I have also seen the opposite when the relationship is right. Many businesspeople have strong business models, good people skills, and effective systems in place, but they can never seem to take their businesses to the next level. Sometimes these people have to take their focus off of their business and realize the problem is at home. You should focus as much energy as you would put into fixing a business issue into fixing your relationships at home. It is crucial.

This principle applies to all of your relationships with others. Anyone you care about has the power to take up time in your head. If you are constantly fighting with someone, maybe it is time to back away from that friendship. Real friendships are supposed to provide real benefits to both sides. If your friendships are having the opposite effect, it may be time to move on and find people who bring joy into your life.

My wife and I used to get together with people I dreaded spending time with. Every time the phone rang, I was hoping these people were calling to say that they were canceling. Eventually, I decided to stop playing the fool and get some friends who I consider to be real friends, who bring fun and relaxation to any gathering. There is no substitute for real friends. You enjoy being around them, they enrich your soul, and they give you the rest and laughter you need to function at maximum capacity at work. Thank God, I am surrounded with real friends now.

With Yourself

Your relationship with yourself is as important, if not more important, than your relationships with others. Everyone wants success, but do you believe that you deserve success? Many people have not asked themselves this question. All they know is that every time they get close, they end up doing something to derail the success they are about to achieve. If you don't believe you deserve success, the question is, "Why?" You need to understand where you are so you know what to do next.

Once you understand the why – whether it's bad decisions you can't get over, or something you did to someone that no one knows about, or your habit of lying – you need to deal with it. Go and apologize to someone if you need to, confess that you did something in the past, or just make the decision to stop lying and to become accountable. You will be amazed at what happens when you get that giant monkey off your back.

I mentioned earlier that when I was a kid, I lived in six different states at different times. Unfortunately, this gave me the opportunity to become whatever I wanted to be in each different state. For some reason, I was ashamed of my poverty. I didn't want anyone to know what I came from or where I lived. More than a few times, I actually had some friends' mothers drop me off at houses a mile or more away from my real home, because I didn't want anyone to know where I lived. For years, I carried around the mindset that people were going to look down on me, and I acted as I did to rise above it all. You can imagine how hard I had to work to keep it up, with one lie after another. I would wash my shoes by hand and put them back in the box they came in everyday to keep them looking new. If I didn't have name-brand shoes, I would wear bigger pants that would cover the logo. Whenever a school trip came up that cost money, I would get angry if someone asked me anything that hinted at the possibility that I wouldn't have the money for the trip. It sounds ridiculous to me now, but this was my reality. I finally got to a place where I realized that everyone else had stuff they were dealing with, too, and I didn't need to be perfect. In fact, perfection was a little annoying to them.

Many of you are still living the lies you have created for yourself. One thing I have learned about people over the years is that everyone can smell a fraud from a mile away. Nobody wants to do business with a fraud, and neither do you. Stop deceiving yourself, wake up, and start brand new. Your business and your life will benefit from your honesty and action.

Emotional Status

Where you are emotionally can be a very tough question to answer. To be successful in business, and in life in general, you have to be a strong, internally stable person. I am not saying that everyone has to have the same personality. If you have ever watched Jim Cramer on CNBC, you probably noticed that he

> *Many people want success but they don't know what success brings.*

tends to present an over-hyperactive attitude, but if you ever speak to him in person, you realize that what you see on television is not necessarily how he acts throughout the day. How could it be? To make good decisions and form good relationships, you have to be able to stop and think about what is going on around you. Could you imagine five Jim Cramers walking into a room and trying to have a conversation with one another? No one would be able to get a word in.

People seem to attract other people who are similar to themselves. I mention this because, in order to succeed in business, people do have to be drawn to you, and they have to want to come back again and again. No business succeeds on one-time customers (with exception of highly-specialized ones, like some medical practices).

The questions to ask yourself about your emotional status are: Can you handle success? Can you handle failure? Can you handle rejection? Do you have the tenacity to push, push, and keep pushing to make success happen for yourself? There are many other questions to be asked but I want you to focus right now on success and then failure.

Many people want success but they don't know what success brings. I mentioned earlier that some people are so comfortable with conflict that, if someone else doesn't cause it, they will. How many True Hollywood Stories have you seen of Stars who attained success too quickly, weren't ready for it, and ended up ruining their lives? Over and over again, you'll hear them say that, once they reached stardom, all they really wanted was their old life back again. They didn't understand that success brings scrutiny, pressure, and expectations.

I know what I'm talking about. My team was just named one of the top two teams in the state of Connecticut in only our second full year in operation; I was given a major award that is usually awarded to gray-haired men; and I just got off the phone with a reporter from an internationally-known magazine who wanted to interview me. When I hung up, I found myself asking, "What is going on here? You are a kid from a broken home. You are nothing special. Have I peaked too soon?" Asking these questions is healthy because they require me to respond. The answers were: What should happen. Yes, it's true. Yes, it's true, again. And absolutely not, I am just getting started. For a moment there, I started to feel the weight of expectations on my shoulders. I am much more comfortable playing the role of the underdog, rather than the favorite. I think it is human nature to want to make someone pleasantly surprised, instead of bitterly disappointed. Either way, once you reach success, you have no choice. You are now expected to deliver at all times, and you have to be ready for what this brings.

The other important question is whether you can handle failure. Many people never even consider the possibility that they could fail in whatever they are doing. Failure for people like this, myself included, is not an option. This is a good mindset to have, as long as you also adopt the idea of expecting the best, but planning for the worst.

Remember, when I started in real estate, I had every intention of succeeding, but I still had money put aside and jobs lined up just in case it didn't work out. It is tough to balance these two ideas, and not every one can do it, because this mindset can be used as an excuse for not succeeding and as an example of a lack of faith. But people who don't adopt this mindset are left with disaster the first time they fail because they have no back- up plan. Consider this: Tiger Woods is the best golfer in the history of the world, but even he has plans just in case he doesn't make the cut for the final two days of the tournament. Do you think he expects to miss the cut? Of course not. But if Tiger Woods can plan just in case he doesn't make the cut, you can surely expect the best and plan for the worst.

If you have asked yourself the above questions, and the answers are not what they should be, hold off on going for the ladder right now. Work on solving your emotional needs and positioning yourself better for success and for failure. You cannot plan for one and not the other and be considered a responsible business person. As I love to say to anyone who is a little off at the moment, "Get your mind right!"

Decision-Making Ability

Depending on your age, where you are right now could be the result of the decisions your parents made or the result of the decisions that you have made over time. Regardless of who made the decision, where you are now has a direct correlation with decisions made in the past. This is encouraging, because it also means that where you are going to be in the future will be a direct result of the decisions you are making today.

They seem to know how to resolve conflicts, and even better, how to avoid unnecessary disputes.

Some people are great decision makers. They just seem to know what to do and when to do it. They know when it is time to invest, or which ventures they should get involved in and which to stay out of. They seem to know how to resolve conflicts, and even better, how to avoid unnecessary disputes. This doesn't mean that they never make a mistake, but overall, they are just great decision makers. Other people tend to want their opinion on what to do and how to do it. Ask yourself: "Do many different people come to me for advice on a fairly consistent basis?" If they do, it is because they feel that you have a measure of wisdom and want to take advantage of your decision-making ability. This is a good place to be.

I am not perfect at it, but I think I can look back and say with a certain level of confidence that I have been a pretty good decision maker. I have always been able to determine how a particular decision will play out long term with a relative amount of accuracy. This is without a doubt one of the largest contributors to my current success. While others have had to spend time fixing their past mistakes before they can move forward, I have been able to focus on the future, because I haven't had to worry as much about past bad decisions. I used to shy away from saying something like that because of how it can sound, but at some point, you need to hear that good decisions lead to good results. Our society so often highlights people who have made bad decisions, but have come back and made something of themselves. Sometimes these people are highlighted so much, we forget that not every good outcome comes from going to prison. I enjoy a good comeback story as much as anyone, and I definitely think they are extremely important for people to hear, but I don't believe that people who got it right the first time get focused on enough. Maybe if we did hear more about people who make good decisions, younger people would have some examples to follow and would know that they can achieve big things without falling on their faces or making terrible decisions early on.

There is another side to this. There are people who seem to make bad decision after bad decision. It doesn't matter how clear cut the situation might be. These people just have a knack for making terrible decisions. It doesn't even have to be a decision as obviously bad as betting their rent on a dog race. It often has more to do with how they spend their time, who they marry, what they buy, what they invest in, or how they handle certain situations.

My advice is to get your decision-making abilities up to par before deciding to start your own business adventure. And it can be an adventure. Making bad decisions in your business affects every other part of your life, as in dominoes. Here is how it goes. Your business isn't profitable so you feel stressed. You have to lay off workers, which adds to their stress and panic. You now have trouble paying your business and personal bills. You get even more stressed and start to fight with your spouse. Your children see you fighting all the time, which takes their toll on them. Eventually, you get divorced due to a lack of finances, which leads to a lack of communication and trust between the two of you. Now your children are in the middle of a custody battle, and they act out by hanging out with the wrong crowd and starting to do drugs. Your seventeen-year-old daughter finds out she is pregnant. She now feels that she has to drop out of high school, because she is too embarrassed to be seen by her peers again. All of this came about because you made bad decisions about your business. Do you see how this can happen? This may sound far-fetched, but I don't believe it is unrealistic to believe that it can happen.

If you are a bad decision maker, how do you fix it? This is not completely simple, but here are three steps you can take to change your patterns of bad decision making.

Step One: Start Making Small Decisions

The first step is to start making small decisions to get your momentum going. Start to get the obvious things right. These types of decisions cover who you spend your time with and how you spend your money. I have found that the majority of people who make bad financial decisions know they are making bad decisions. They just get caught up in the "I want" mentality, instead of the "I need" mentality. So start now, and begin to make wise decisions about your finances. Start to take small amounts of your income, or more if possible, and learn to save, give, and pay off debt. You need to do this consistently for about 3-6 months. I've heard it said that it takes 28 days to form a habit, but I suggest giving yourself more time.

Step Two: Take on Bigger Decisions

After you have mastered small decisions, take on bigger ones, such as where you will work or who you will hire. At this time, you should be conservative with your decision making. I understand that highly successful people do take risks, but this is not the time. When you are looking at your options for a particular decision, don't consider the upside of each option, but decide which option has a positive outlook with the least amount of risk. Remember, you are trying to establish a new foundation for good decision making by getting base hits. You are not trying to hit home runs at this point because you cannot afford to strike out right now. Give yourself another 3-6 months for this period. This may seem like a long time, but when you consider how much you have to learn, it is really not that long, at all.

Step Three: Review and Analyze

After you have completed these two periods, you will enter the final phase, which is called the review and analyze phase. Start by listing all of the decisions you have made over the past 6-12 months on a piece of paper. (Note that it may help for you to keep a record of these decisions while you are going through the first two steps.) Then, one-by-one, begin to analyze how those decisions panned out. Did you put more money in your savings than ever before? Did you give away more money? Did you pay off more debt to get yourself into a position of strength so you could run your business effectively? Are the people you are spending more time with adding joy to your life or adding stress to it? Is your current job working out, or are the employees you hired productive members of your company? If you made decisions as conservatively as you were supposed to, you should like the answers to these questions.

I have found that success and positive results are fulfilling and leave you wanting more. You now have the foundation you need and have made good decisions for long enough to be ready to march on and do what you are called to do. If you read the domino scenario I laid out above and saw the bad effects it had on that family's life, imagine now the effects that good decisions will have on you and your family.

Finances

Your financial status is probably the easiest of the four to measure. It is the most tangible one, because you can actually record how much you are spending, how much you are bringing in, and how much you have saved and invested. I think this is the area most overlooked by entrepreneurs considering starting or running a business. Maybe they don't want to face the truth about their finances, or they know the truth is bad, or they know the truth is great and they have nothing to worry about, or they just assume things will work out.

Whenever you embark on any sort of business adventure that doesn't guarantee any kind of salary or income, you really need to have a minimum of three months worth (I prefer six months worth) of living expenses in a readily-available account. These expenses include housing, transportation, food, and other necessary expenditures. You also need to know that if you use this money up, you will still be able to make your way. If the money you are calling your living-expense money is really coming out of your retirement account, you really do not have sufficient savings.

I have seen many people with great ideas and lots of energy go into business, but fail shortly afterwards, because they could not keep up with their expenses. Many successful businesses do not see a profit for two years. Sometimes, it takes time to gain market share, regardless of how great your idea. Consider Ted Turner. It was years before he saw a profit on two business ventures: the TBS television channel and the Atlanta Braves major league baseball team. But he knew that this would be the case when he purchased them and was prepared for it. Both ventures are now highly profitable. Remember this when starting your own venture. You have to consider your carrying costs and your overhead, no matter how great your idea seems to be. Even the greatest ideas can fail for lack of foresight, bad planning, and bad decisions. This is why some of the most talented building contractors I have ever met fail in running their own business. They might be great contractors, but they don't fully understand how to run a business and how to handle finances.

The most basic principle in the financial world is to have more coming in than going out. Yet, many people don't understand this. Before you decide to start a business, make an effort to get and keep your personal finances in order first. I understand that this isn't something that really excites you, but I am more interested in giving you the basics that lead to your success than exciting you, sending you out, and having you come back more broken than you were before.

If you have reviewed these four categories and feel that you are in pretty good shape with each one of them, you are probably ready to start building your own business or growing your current business. If you feel that you fall short in one or more of these categories, you can fix them over time. Take the time you need to do things right. For many of you, it may be a while before you are able to move forward, but it is better to start off right and succeed than to start off too soon and fail. Don't become the statistic that you don't want to be.

Chapter 3

Projecting Your Future

Imagine yourself getting up in the morning, giddy about your prospects for the day and actually excited about going to work. You get out of the shower and are greeted with a full bacon-and-eggs breakfast. There is fresh coffee waiting for you at the table and another cup waiting for you in a thermos for when you leave. You eat your food and it is cooked to perfection. As you are getting ready to leave, your spouse kisses you good-bye, looks you in the eye with pure joy, and can't wait for you to come home. As you head to the door, your kids come running over to hug you. They have smiles on their faces that would melt a snowman. You tell them how you are going to come home after work and take a walk with them around the neighborhood. You can tell by their expressions that they will look forward to that walk all day long.

You go to work and find that your assistant has taken it upon herself to show up early and has been proactively setting up appointments for you. She hands you your schedule for the day and tells you about any messages. You return the calls, decide to have lunch with an old client, and set a date to go golfing with another old friend so you can talk about possible deals.

At 1:00 p.m., the mail arrives, and there is a check in it for $35,000. You feel a small thrill of excitement because you realize that this one check is more than you used to make in a full year and that you are on track to hit your goal of making over $1,000,000 this year. This inspires you to check on some of your other projects, and you find that you made several thousands of dollars overnight from another business you started to generate income online. (I'll talk more about this in Chapter 10: Developing Multiple Streams of Income.) To make matters even better, your financial planner calls to give you an update – your portfolio has increased over 30% this year! It is only mid-day and you have already had enough good news for a month.

Your workload is moving along nicely and you decide to call it a day early and head home to fulfill your promise to your kids and take them for a walk. When you get home, you are greeted once again by a family that is elated to see you, and you start to get ready for your walk. While getting ready, you also make the decision to take your family out to dinner so your spouse doesn't have to cook.

Over dinner, your spouse tells you how he/she was looking online and saw some great bargains on trips to all-inclusive kid-friendly resorts in the Dominican Republic. You decide to book a 10-day vacation without having to check in with anybody. You make your own schedule and won't have a problem paying for this vacation. Not only is the vacation affordable, but the flights are free because you have planned well and have enough airline miles to get tickets for everyone in your family at no cost. Life is good and you know it!

It sounds pretty good, right? It does to me. The reason I put this fantasy in the book is that this is exactly how you have to think. You have to learn to picture what you want your life to look like, no matter how impossible it seems. When I was growing up watching my mother use food stamps to get groceries, do you think I ever imagined a life like what I described above? You bet I did!

Projecting Your Financial Future

I was always a dreamer. I would picture what I wanted my life to look like one week from that day. After that, I would picture five years in the future, 10 years in the future, 20 years in the future, and so on. More importantly, I would perpetually meditate on how I was going to get there. It is the 'getting there' that is important. Our society is filled with dreamers, but not enough doers. Highly successful people have an uncanny ability to predict the future accurately and make decisions in the present that will get them to where they want to be.

This ability to predict the future does not take supernatural power, and you don't have to be able to talk to ghosts from the past. You simply have to be able to forecast human nature (including your own), the overall climate around you, your own strengths and weaknesses, and your driving passion for what you are doing.

Many times I lie awake at night in another world. Nighttime is when I live in the realm of my own reality. Many of you know exactly what I am talking about. Whenever any opportunity presents itself and I deem it worth going after, I will lie awake night after night planning how it will all work out. It consumes me. Not to the point where my family thinks I have lost my marbles, but more than I would ever admit to anyone, if I wanted them to continue to think of me as a sane human being.

When I got into real estate, I lived many parts of my days in this separate world within my mind. I think I had to. If I had focused only on the walls and obstacles around me, I would have given up right from the start. Why put so much effort into something that statistically has almost no chance at survival? The statistics say that the survival rate of a new realtor in the first two years is a little less than 50%; that the average age of a successful realtor is 52, more than double my age at the time; and that it takes a good agent over 10 years to build a successful referral-based business. Here I was entering the business at the age of 22, with no prior experience in running my own business and no contacts in industries that could lead to a lot of referral business. To put it simply, I was a nobody. Undoubtedly, I would become the Managing Member in the club of the over-50% -who-didn't-make-it-in-the-first-two-years. When you add into the equation the facts that I already had a good job, was married, and had plenty of bills, it probably didn't make sense for me to change careers, especially for one that didn't even offer a salary.

I was probably too naïve to understand that the odds were against me. In reality, I think I did know the odds, I just didn't think that they applied to me. In my head, I had worked in the world of real estate for years and everything worked out pretty well for me. I could already see what my billboards would look like and what kinds of direct mail pieces I would mail out. I could even see myself up on stage accepting my lifetime achievement award. I might have been getting ahead of myself, but I could see it all.

Dreaming like this has helped me over the years to keep my eye on the prize. Find something that you want to achieve and start to meditate on it so much that it becomes real to you. You have to feel that not achieving your goal is like having someone literally take what is yours right from your hands. It has to be that real to you. This is not how most people think, but it is this uncommon thinking that creates uncommon results.

The first thing I did was study the other people in the real estate office I was going to work at. I noticed distinct differences between those who seemed to do a lot of business and those who did not. I noticed the very successful agents always seemed to be on the phone or communicating with someone. The ones who didn't appear to have much business, tended to be sitting at their desks thinking about dinner or talking to their spouses about the weekend. The message was loud and clear. I needed to be on the phone or writing an email from day one, communicating with as many people as I could about my new real estate career.

The second thing I noticed was how the successful realtors dressed. They seemed to be dressed as if they worked at a corporation. They looked as if they were the head of the company. The others seemed to wear jeans and shorts and other casual items. They looked more as if they were running errands and decided to stop in to do a little business, instead of the other way around.

The last thing I noticed was how knowledgeable the more successful agents were about what was going on in the market and with real estate in general. You could tell that they breathed this industry. This was all I needed to know to begin to form this world in my head and strategize how I was going to become a real estate success.

Starting that night, I went home and I pictured myself on the phone with potential clients. I pictured what questions they would ask me and how I would answer. I pictured myself having lunch meetings with other professionals, trying to make alliances with them that would turn into reciprocal referral business. I pictured myself writing up offers for people and having them accepted. How would the other agent respond to our offer, and how would I negotiate in the best interest of my client? These are important questions that are better not handled on the fly. If you are in the middle of negotiations and the other party asks you a question or brings up a point that you are not prepared for, you are finished. In chess they refer to this as 'checkmate.'

Understanding human nature also meant that I had to be able to forecast how my co-workers would respond to my success. Many people get used to their position at the top and don't like some new guy/gal coming into their domain and demonstrating that there is a new sheriff in town. It is like an old western when John Wayne walks through the swinging doors into the bar and everyone looks at the newcomer. They are wondering, "Who is this? What is he doing in my bar? Who does he think he is?" Inevitably, it ends up in a shootout outside the bar because there is room for only one top dog.

I sincerely hope you don't challenge your coworkers to a shootout, but you do need to understand how they will feel and how they will react. In my situation, because I knew I would be successful and that various feelings would arise in the office, I decided to be diplomatic from the start. No, you don't have to act fake and pretend to be nice to everyone, but you should want to be nice to everyone because they are your peers and because you want to have good, strong relationships with them. They are only being human when they begin to resent you and your success, especially if you are significantly younger and less experienced than they are. Understanding this will help you to anticipate their feelings and deal with them before they even arise.

I made it a point to have conversations with people in my office and form bonds while I was still relatively unsuccessful. Over time, I would ask the more successful agents questions about the business and lean on them for advice in many different situations. When you give seasoned veterans the honor and respect they deserve, you disarm them in a way. How could they want to see me fail when they had invested so much into my success? They had taken the time to share their expert advice with me. If I failed, it would mean that their advice was wasted. Do you see how this works? When you form these types of bonds, the very people who might have been secretly hoping for your failure, find themselves rooting for your success because they are a part of it. Not only did I gain their experience and wisdom, but I also gained their respect and friendship. It became a win-win for everyone involved. To this day, I find myself now returning the favor and trying to help other Realtors to have the same success that I have had, or even more.

One of the most important issues I prepared for was questions about my youth. No matter how polished I had become or how knowledgeable I tried to be, I was still a young kid in the eyes of many others. When you are young, you need to realize that you are constantly starting out as the underdog in any business transaction you do. People want to deal with others who are mature, credible, smart, committed, and competent enough to handle their business. I was not selling shoes anymore. Now I was selling properties worth hundreds of thousands or even millions of dollars, and a lot was on the line. One screw-up could cost my client more money than I had ever seen in my life. This has been a factor for me even up to today. Many of my clients call me to set up an appointment because they have heard of me. When we finally meet in person, I can see them wondering, "How could this young guy be the person I heard about? He can't possibly have done the things that my friend told me he had done." I get so frustrated that I have to continually prove myself, even though I have higher sales volumes, higher commissions, and more transactions than the majority of my colleagues. When will my resume speak for itself?

One way to meet this head on is to dress like a successful person. Even when I wasn't yet quite the success I wanted to be, the one thing I could control was the image that I projected to other people. So I mixed and matched pants and blazers, shirts and ties, and shoes and belts to make it appear as if I had more outfits than I really had.

I learned to be a bit of a chameleon as well. If my client was a hard-working blue-collar kind of a guy, I knew there was nothing he would hate more than some polished white-collar real estate agent kid. But if my client was an intellectual, corporate vice-president type, then my image, my speech, and my mannerisms had to change to make him feel more comfortable. This really applies to all age groups.

If you can get your clients to see beyond your age and inexperience, they will actually find themselves rooting for you to succeed. They will feel as if they had a part in discovering you and had something to do with your success. This is an important point. If you prove to them that you are just as knowledgeable as your competitor with 20 years of experience, but you are hungrier and have more drive, your clients will feel that they have found something special and that they have a duty to work with you because they don't want to miss out on the opportunity. How many people would have hired Picasso to paint their family portrait if they knew what he was to become? How many people would have became golf buddies with Tiger Woods when he was a kid if they knew he would become the greatest golfer of all time? This is how you have to think and project yourself. Your clients have to feel as if they are working with the next great in your industry.

Many people jump into project after project, deal after deal, opportunity after opportunity, and they never seem to do anything that is long lasting or that matters. Every time you see them, they are excited about a new job, or they are selling something unbelievable, or they are dating "The One." We all know people like this. Some of us are these people. There is an aspect of these people that is admirable: They want to be successful and they have the zeal for success. They just don't have the ingredients. Everyone wants

Everyone wants the warm bread and butter but no one wants to knead the dough.

the warm bread and butter but no one wants to knead the dough. People like this want to be successful so badly that they are willing to chase after every counterfeit that comes across their path. It's the old saying: "If it seems too good to be true, it probably is."

I really believe that if something can be built easily, it can come down easily. I respect people who don't go after every opportunity. For the most part, if people can be talked into something, they can just as easily be talked out of it. The point of all of this is to say that you need to investigate opportunities a little more thoroughly before making a 'leap of faith.' In fact, when you make your leap of faith, it shouldn't be blind faith. It should be a calculated, researched leap of faith.

When I decided to go into real estate, I had a very promising job. I was making good money, the company was paying for my car and gas, and I had flexibility, which I loved. There was no real reason to leave, except for the fact that I did not love what I did and I knew there was something bigger out there for me. I'd like to say that I just decided to take up real estate and left my old job behind me, but that is not reality. In the real world, you have mortgages or rent, you have car payments, you have cable and phone bills, you have utility bills, and you have to buy food. If I had focused on what was holding me back, I never could have focused on where I was going.

This is why you have to understand the climate around you. At that time, the real estate market was booming and the economy was just as strong. I was getting offered a new job almost every week, without ever sending out my resume. Although it was a risk to take up real estate as a career, it was a calculated risk. I knew that I had enough money in savings and equity that I could give real estate the shot it deserved for about six months without missing a payment on any of my bills. If it didn't work out, I could either take one of these other jobs or possibly get hired back at my old company.

Many of you reading those last sentences will say that I wasn't committed enough to making my career in real estate work. I simply disagree. You can fully commit yourself without being foolish, and it is foolish to commit yourself without having a plan to support your family. I like to say that you plan for the worst, but believe for the best. This mindset allows you to take chances, but not at the expense of those who depend on you to provide for them. You will never reach your full potential or do anything larger than yourself if you never take chances. If you want to be like everyone else, then just do what everyone else does.

All of this sounds great, but I knew that I needed my wife on board for this huge decision and needed a plan in case I failed so we would still be okay. I discussed all of these points with my wife and told her that I believed that real estate was part of my calling. I explained that you are never as successful in some random job as you could be in what you are supposed to be doing. I truly believe that to this day. I laid out the finances, showed her that we were in a position to take the risk, and told her that I believed this was the right thing to do. This is how business and family are intertwined. If I didn't have a strong relationship with my wife, she never would have trusted me to make such a life-changing decision. But she not only trusted me, she supported me. The difference between your spouse's trust and your spouse's support can be the difference between you just getting by and you making it big. If your spouse trusts you, you will be able to try things and hope they work out; but you can't really tell him or her when things are not going so well, because he or she will always be waiting for the other shoe to fall and thinking that it is only a matter of time before you go back to your old job. But if your spouse supports you, you can have a bad day and still know he or she is going to encourage you and push you forward. In this case, your spouse isn't even thinking that your old job is an option because he or she is so sure that you are going to succeed at what you are doing. Which would you rather have?

Knowing that my wife had my back no matter what gave me the confidence to fail. I knew that if I failed, our relationship would remain strong, and that meant the world to me. I am eternally grateful.

I knew that my strengths blended in perfectly with real estate and that my weaknesses were things that I could fix so they wouldn't affect my real estate career. I also knew that the overall climate and timing was perfect and that the upside of a real estate career was far beyond any success I had already achieved. The possibilities were endless.

The last ingredient I needed was a passion for the business – and I already had it. When I was a kid, I was my mother's part-time, unpaid real estate assistant, and I loved it! I loved the flexibility she had. I loved the potential for income that she had. I loved that there was no ceiling on her income and that her success or failure rested squarely on her shoulders. I had already been dabbling in real estate as an investment because, even though it wasn't my job yet, I just had to be a part of it. I loved real estate and what it had to offer.

If you go through a thought process similar to the one I've just outlined and everything adds up but you don't have a passion for the opportunity, go back to the drawing board because when things get tough, and they will, you will have a built-in excuse to give up. Nor will you stay up at night picturing and strategizing how you are going to do something, if you don't have a passion for it.

Projecting Your Family Life

When projecting your future, you want to be sure that your business goals don't collide with your personal goals. Think about it. If you want to be a mother of three children and attend PTA meetings and go on field trips with your children, it may not make sense to pay an exorbitant amount of money on law school and become an attorney. You may reach your goal of becoming an attorney, but something may eventually have to give. If you do have children one day and decide to be very active in their lives, you may have to abandon your law career, which would leave you with hundreds of thousands of dollars of student loan debts and little to show for it. These are the types of situations that you have to learn to forecast in your head when making your decisions. We are going to discuss this a little more in another chapter, but the ability to forecast your future with precision is a skill you will need to learn to maximize your success in this life.

Your business and personal life are most definitely intertwined. If more highly successful people recognized this fact, you would see less business people lock themselves in their offices because they have no desire to go home. Truly successful people have balance in their lives and don't find comfort in staying away from their family. Or even worse, you read about successful business people committing suicide over incidents or mistakes that have occurred on the job. This wouldn't happen if these same people had proper priorities in their lives. It is my opinion that focusing on one area of your life without equally focusing on the other is a form of suicide. You are making the decision that, in order for you to be truly successful, something in your life has to die to make room for the other. I don't see business and personal as an either/or type of decision. You can have both.

On the flip side, it is the reason that you can speak with a family man or woman and they sound extremely happy until you get into the financial aspect of their lives. It is then that you feel the mountain of anxiety flow off of them because they love their family dearly but really are not sure how to provide for them in the years to come. Many of these people, especially in today's times, are one layoff away from disaster. You can be the greatest business mind alive, but still have your home budget out of order and be on the brink of foreclosure or bankruptcy. Or even worse, you don't even have a budget at home. It always amazes me how people that have great systems in place at work and run very successful businesses don't apply the same principles at home.

If you are reading this book and you don't have a spouse and children at home, understand that most likely someday you will. Now is the time to use that forward thinking, that projection, I talked about earlier. Understand that the same principles that will work for your family someday are the ones you should be practicing now in your work life and in your relationship with the people closest to you.

Business is all about relationships and budgets, planning ahead, setting goals, and achieving them. Your home is no different. The only difference is that you truly love the people at home and have a vested interest in their success. I am not suggesting that you treat your house like a business and decide you want to layoff your spouse when things get rough, or reorganize and send one of your children to another family. But you should look at your spouse as your partner in every aspect of your home life. Just as you wouldn't make major decisions at work without consulting your 50% partner, the same should apply at home. Your kids are executives in the making. You are teaching them how to run successful households as well. They will need to learn the value of healthy relationships and boundaries and proper respect for money. They should never feel that anything is free. There is a price for everything. While everything is attainable, you have to work hard enough to earn it. Could you imagine a CEO of a company constantly buying his or her employees different perks without some sense of that employee earning it, just because the company had a good year. I think that subconsciously those employees would learn over time to stop valuing these perks and would come to expect them. The same principles apply at home to a lesser extent. Obviously you want to bless your children and bless your spouse to the best of your ability. I am just trying to bring you to a higher understanding where you question and understand why you do everything you do. One of the characteristics of highly successful people is that they don't waste their decisions. They know why they make the decisions they make and are ready to accept the consequences for those decisions because of that.

The Number One Lesson

If you can learn to take this same approach when making decisions, you will find that you waste a lot less time doing things that don't really matter or that should never have been done in the first place. You will also find that you will not do as many things that are merely good, because you would rather spend your time doing things that are going to lead you to greatness. I could have made the decision to take one of those other job offers and I would have made more money than I was making at the time, which sounds pretty good. Instead, I decided to use the technique of projecting the future in my head and figure out which was the great option, not just the good option. Good options present themselves regularly. Great options have to be pursued.

> *The Number One Lesson I want you to learn from what I'm saying is: Do not deceive yourself. Self-deception is worse in my mind than being an evil person.*

The Number One Lesson I want you to learn from what I'm saying is: Do not deceive yourself. Self-deception is worse in my mind than being an evil person. For the most part, the majority of evil people at least know they are evil. Self-deceived people motor on with their daily lives without ever wanting to make any changes, because they aren't even aware that anything is wrong. Even worse, they risk hurting and deceiving others in the process.

Now may be time for you to do an audit of yourself to understand where you are in life. You may have been deceiving yourself for years and no one has had the courage to tell you so;

or maybe people have told you and you just wouldn't listen. God only gives us one life to live. Wouldn't it be a shame to live your whole life deceiving yourself?

It is only when you learn to forecast human nature, understand the climate around you, know your strengths and weaknesses, and have a passion for what you are doing that you can be on the road to making better and more profitable lifetime decisions. These decisions will affect not only you, but your family and others as well. They deserve the attention to get them right.

Chapter 4

Why You Need to Have Motives, Purposes, and Passion in Your Business and Your Life

Like almost every other person on this planet, I am on Facebook. One of the features of Facebook is that your friends update their statuses throughout the day, and you, as their friend, get to see their updates. One of the common themes of these updates is how much so many of my friends do not like their jobs. On Tuesday afternoons, they are counting down to the weekend or counting down until closing time, and then they start all over again the next day.

I can't criticize my Facebook friends too much, because I understand what it feels like to always look forward to being anywhere but where you currently are, especially at work. Luckily, I don't feel that way anymore. I genuinely enjoy my job and look forward to being in the office, dealing with a client, or speaking to a group of professionals. About the only thing I don't enjoy on a regular basis is saying goodbye to my kids every morning.

This is not because I am some kind of 'mind wizard' and have become one with myself. It is simply because I have made a decision that I only get one life and one shot at living my life the way that I want to live it, and I am not going to waste it always wishing I was doing something else. If you truly feel as if you are supposed to be doing something else, why not take steps now to put yourself in a position to be doing whatever it is in the very near future?

I act on two principles that have made my days not only more enjoyable, but also more productive. The first principle is

Passion gets you through when you want to give up.

that I have a motive for every single thing I do and every single person I talk to during the day. You could easily substitute 'purpose' for 'motive', but I think 'motive' drives the point home more clearly. This doesn't mean you are not genuine, but you should know *why*

you are doing something and expect some type of result from every single task you do and every single conversation you engage in.

The second principle is passion. There is absolutely no substitute for passion. Passion gets you through when you want to give up. In some cases, it blinds you when you should give up, but if you are on the right track, that can be a good thing. I have countless stories of life successes that, when looking back, just didn't look like they would ever or should ever happen. All of the chips were stacked against me and the odds seemed impossible. Have you ever thought about something you have accomplished and said to yourself, "If I had to do it again and knew it would be this hard, I wouldn't have done it?" The fact that you were able to do it is an example of passion in action working in your life.

Motives

For some reason, there is a perception in our culture that having motives disqualifies you or makes you a less-than-honest person. I don't buy into this perception, because I believe that you actually should have a motive for just about everything you do. It doesn't make much sense for a business person to do anything without knowing why you are there or what you hope to gain. Whether you realize it or not, you already have motives for everything you do.

When you call someone on the phone, you rarely just want to say 'hello' or see how they are doing. Most of the time, you want to get information or ask a question. When you have a meeting with someone at work, it is because you want something out of that meeting – a raise from your boss or clarification of a company policy. Either way, you have a motive.

To go into any business conversation without having a motive is a silly waste of time. I can just about guarantee you that the person on the other side has a motive. I want you to become more aware of your day-to-day activities. If you don't understand why you are speaking with or meeting with a particular person, you will find yourself feeling frustrated and as if you haven't accomplished anything. If you aim at nothing, you are sure to hit it. Just as you set goals for yourself, set an agenda for the day, and then make it a point to carry out that agenda from the moment you start working until the moment you stop. Every person you come in contact with has the potential to assist you in achieving your agenda. Your job is to figure out how.

Please don't misinterpret what I'm saying and become the person that nobody likes or enjoys being around because they "always have a motive." It is important to understand the spirit of what I am saying. You always want to be genuine in every conversation, but you also need to understand *why* you are speaking with people and *what* you hope to get out of it. Sometimes, your motives can be as simple as gaining a little knowledge or enjoying time with that person. The point I am trying to drive home is that you will be much more productive when you know why you are doing something in both your business and personal life. Could you imagine going shopping without having a list of what you need? You would just wander from aisle to aisle, hoping to see something that you wanted, and ultimately buy a lot of junk that you didn't intend to get. Unfortunately, this is how most people treat their daily lives, wandering from conversation to conversation, from person to person, from meeting to meeting, with no real motives.

Passion

You hear it over and over again from highly successful people: If you want to be successful, do what you love to do.

When I decided to go into real estate, I had a good paying job and a matching retirement fund, and I worked for a company that paid for my gas and car. There was only one problem: I wasn't passionate about what I was doing. I enjoyed my job and I really liked the group of people that I was working with, but real estate was my passion and I knew it. There is only one thing worse than being stuck in a bad job, and that is being stuck in a good job. At least, when you are stuck in a bad job, you know that you are not following your true calling and purpose in your life. But when you are stuck in a good job, it is not always as clear whether you are in the right place in your life or not. I don't recommend quitting your job without a plan, but I do recommend doing an audit of your life and figuring out if you are doing what you love. If you are not,

Sometimes the easier decision is not the right one.

there is no better time than now to take the steps necessary to begin putting your life on the track you want it to be on, slowly but surely. Every little step is a step closer than you were a moment ago. Doing what you love will make you happier and usually more successful than you have ever been. There is a difference between completing a task because it is your job and completing a task because it is your passion. Imagine if your passion became your job. It is not impossible.

I used to watch the president of the company I was working for at the time, and a little part of me wanted what he had. I wanted to make good money and make the big decisions that affected whether the company would grow or become stagnant. It would have been a lot easier to have stayed on that path and worked my way up in the company until I found myself in his position. Instead, I decided to follow my passion and do what I love for a living. I now find myself making more money than the president of my former company did, I have more flexibility within my schedule, and more importantly I enjoy going to work everyday. Sometimes the easier decision is not the right one. Follow your gut. Don't get stuck in a dead-end job unless you feel that you are supposed to be there for a specific purpose. You only get one life, so you might as well enjoy it!

Chapter 5

Is Your Faith a Steering Wheel or a Spare Tire?

I was ten years old and sitting in a room full of people. At the time, I was the starting guard on my AAU basketball team and was sitting next to the other starting guard on my squad. Our coach was in the front of the room speaking to the crowd. My friend and I were listening, but we were more interested in the intense tic-tac-toe game we were playing. After this gathering, everyone in the room headed outside for a picnic and softball game. Any guess where we were at the moment? If you guessed "Church," you are right. My basketball coach was the pastor of my church. This made a lasting impression on me, because I had always viewed 'religious people' as idiots, who didn't have anything better to do with their lives. Seeing my cool basketball coach leading a church changed my thinking.

I was like many kids, who at a young age dreaded having to wake up on Sunday morning to go to church. Not so much because I hated church, but because I went to bed late on Saturday night. Every week, I hoped that my mother would see that church wasn't necessary this Sunday, so I could experience true heaven on earth – sleeping in. I was really the easy one in my household. My older brother had to have water poured over his head on more than one occasion to wake him up, but he did go to church on Sunday mornings.

I am not telling this story to push a particular religion or set of beliefs. I have never wanted to cram anything down someone else's throat. I believe that you have more influence over someone when they invite your input or ask for your opinion. The truth, though, is that I would not be genuine if I wrote in detail about living a successful life and left out the Creator of all things.

I have taken a different approach to God. A recent survey said that over 90% of Americans believe in God in one form or another. Out of those 90%, the majority say that they pray to God at least once a week. Yet, if you think about our culture, we are really very much a secular society, and many people follow their religious traditions only so they don't make God angry. To really grasp this concept, think about what happens when someone close to you gets sick. Who do you call on? If you were on a plane that was going down, you better believe that you would become the equivalent of Billy Graham in an instant, with prayers coming out of your mouth. This is where I try to be different. I have always really tried to view God more as my steering wheel than my spare tire. I mean that I don't just call on God when I'm stuck. I try to call on Him before I get stuck, so maybe I can avoid getting stuck to begin with.

> *I believe that you have more influence over someone when they invite your input or ask for your opinion.*

Some are taught to see God as an angry God waiting to punish you, but that was never my perspective. When my first son was born, my views towards the idea of a Creator changed even more. I now see God as a father. Not an abusive, overly tense father, but a loving, forgiving, want-the-best-for-you kind of father. This was not easy for me, because I grew up without a father. The love I immediately had for my son, which has only grown with time, probably doesn't even compare to the love of God for me and my family. Knowing this, I really try to be different about the way I do things because, just as a child wants to make his or her father proud, I take the same approach in my relationship with God and with everything that I do on a daily basis.

I have always tried to understand God from the viewpoint of an intellectual. Thinking in this way, I came to the conclusion that it was healthy to understand that there is something greater than myself and that the effect that the pull of the moon has on the exact timing of the waves of the ocean didn't happen by accident. When thinking about it, I found that it took a lot more faith to believe that everything in the universe happened by accident than it did to believe that there is a Supreme Being who created it all and lined everything up. There are still the silly questions that I want to ask God when I leave this earth, such as, "Can you create a rock large enough so not even you can move it?" and things like that. But they are just that, silly. From an intellectual perspective (and taking faith out of it,, for the moment), I guess I just came to the conclusion that, if I believed and acted as if there is a God and was wrong, the consequences would be far less than if I believed and acted as if there was no God and was wrong.

There are three things that finding something or someone greater than myself have done for me, and could do for you, too, no matter what religion you subscribe to: It keeps me humble, gives me a different perspective, and keeps me sane and confident.

Keeps Me Humble

When you reach a certain level of success, you will have to avoid many pitfalls. Pitfall number one is undoubtedly Pride. If you pay attention to our current movie stars, you will notice that most of them are full of self-pride. It would be easy to criticize these people as selfish and arrogant, and in some cases they are, but I have always tried to look at *why* people are the way they are and to understand where they are coming from. This is a good perspective to have in any endeavor, but it's especially important in business. Judgmental people usually don't get very far. When you try to see things from the stars' perspectives, their attitudes almost make sense. They have paparazzi following them around all the time. They can get paid simply for allowing photography of their family. They have bodyguards traveling with them to keep people away. When they do go to events, they almost always walk down a red carpet, get interviewed, pose for pictures, have countless fans screaming their names and crying in many cases, and make millions of dollars. When you look at it this way, you can start to see why it is easy for stars to believe their own press clippings. In a way, it is similar to being a parent. When you tell your child who they are all the time and reinforce what you expect from them, they tend to become that in the long term. Many stars and celebrities are merely reacting in the same way.

I use the example of movie stars, not because I have ever experienced anything close to the life of a celebrity, but because

I have felt it on a smaller scale. When I first started in real estate, I was literally a nobody. I didn't have contacts or clients or references, nothing. After winning Rookie-of-the-Year my first year and putting up very high numbers my second year, I started to notice a shift in the way that people perceived and reacted to me. My intuition was proven recently when I was told by an associate of mine that until he got to know me, he thought I changed my clothing in a telephone booth like Superman. I hope he now knows the truth. People are people, and while some are more dynamic than others, everyone still puts on their pants one leg at a time.

It was very tempting to get a big head when I noticed how people perceived me and were talking to me. This is where it is important to recognize that there is Someone greater than yourself. Just when I almost became full of myself, I realized that I am really not all that great myself. I am really just a kid from a lower middle class family, who happens to be blessed with a certain set of God-given abilities. I know that ultimately God determines who gets what, and if he decided to give me the abilities I am benefiting from today, the real credit actually goes to him. My mother used to remind me that, if someone gives something to you, they can take it away as well. I believe this and am conscious of it, and it tends to humble me when I want to take great credit for something. This is not easy to do, but it is a lot easier than waking up one day and realizing that you do not like the person that you have become. I am fully aware of this reality and refuse to get to that place, and you should as well.

Gives Me a Different Perspective

If you ever watched the television show *Married With Children*, you probably remember the title character, Al Bundy. There was almost nothing that Al loved to do more than sit around and tell stories about his good old days playing high school football. According to him, it was amazing that he did not get drafted right out of high school into the NFL. He seemed to score a touchdown every time he touched the ball.

Because I'm around so many business people every day, I hear these kinds of stories all the time. Usually after people are finished with their old sports stories, they shift to the negotiations where they just got the deal of a lifetime. They got everything they wanted and more, and then got the price lowered right before they closed on the house or picked up their new car, or whatever it is that they are talking

> *Did you ever stop to think that a good deal is one that is good for both parties?*

about. There was a time when I heard these stories and started to take part, too. There is nothing inherently wrong about this, but I want to introduce you to a different perspective.

Did you ever stop to think that a good deal is one that is good for both parties? Think about it: If you truly got everything you wanted and made the deal of a lifetime, the other party was ripped off or raked over the coals. Lately, I have tried to see things from God's perspective and think about what He considers a good deal to be. Try to do this yourself, and you'll see that it can actually be very beneficial for you. If someone knows that when they negotiate with you, you are going to try to take them for everything they have, they may decide that it is not worth doing business with you at all. In other words, you may make a one-time great deal, but true success is in the long term. Your reputation is everything in business and in life in general. I'm not suggesting that you go easy when negotiating, but when people start to understand that you are tough and do your homework, *but are fair*, they will respect you more and want to do business with you for life.

To understand this perspective, look at it from a higher point of view. If you agree with what I said earlier about God loving me and my family, how could you not also believe that He loves the person sitting across the table from you? Many times those people have children, bills, and responsibilities just like you. I believe this is one of the things that separates me from the pack. Anybody can learn how to speak to people and run a business efficiently. But not everyone can take on this unique perspective, because it may mean that you will have to forego some short-term gains to do what is right. That is not always easy to do in the moment.

Keeps Me Sane and Confident

Have you ever had an unbelievably crazy day where everything seemed to go wrong? I have. On days like that, I will ask myself question after question in my head about whether I made a bad decision or mismanaged something. *Not* whether God did it to me, but whether a poor decision I made is just playing out its natural course. Bad decisions tend to lead to chaos. Whenever this happens and I am able to sit back and relax at the end of the day, I am comforted by the idea that God is still on His throne. I like the saying, "This too shall pass."

Having Faith does something else for me as well: It gives me confidence. That may sound strange, but when I look back over my life, I can see His handprint all over it. I can see why certain events took place in my life, even though times may not have been great or I questioned why God let something happen. This gives me confidence now, because I trust that whatever I am going through will work out in the end. It always has and I believe it always will. I'm not saying it will work out the way I want it to, but it will work out. That is the difference between playing God and letting God have His way. I don't always have to know exactly how something will work out, but I do know He has my best interests in mind when I am doing everything I can to do things the right way. I have been called many worse things in my life than an 'optimist.'

I am fully aware that some readers will think I am naïve for believing that there is a God looking over me and planning my life. I cannot blame them. I was turned off for years by religious people who used God as a crutch. Everything good or bad that happened to them was because of God. While many things happen because of God, I do not discount the role that we play, as well. Earlier, I mentioned the specific gifts He gave me, and I am sure that He gave you special gifts, as well. Even with these gifts, we are still personally responsible for doing with them what we will. God doesn't do for us what we can do for ourselves. A God who acts as a nurse is not one I'd want to relate to. A nurse can come to your house and take care of you and tell you what to wear and how to do your hair – but this is not what God does. We all have the responsibility to do

> *God doesn't do for us what we can do for ourselves.*

what we will with the talents that God has given us. I personally count on God for the things that I can't do; an example is setting up a divine meeting with a contact I would never have been able to get on the phone, but somehow we end up pumping gas next to each other and begin to talk. The next thing you know this contact will either open doors for me that I couldn't have opened for myself or put me in contact with someone who can do the same. This has been happening my whole life, and I can't take credit for it.

Part II

Skills and Attitudes for Success

Chapter 6

Managing Time Wisely and Working Efficiently

It is clear that one of the most important reasons why many businesses don't prosper is because of one thing: Poor time management. This is the same reason why so many people's lives are always so stressful and why they don't feel as if they ever get enough rest.

I have always wondered how some people could be so smart, so practical, and so good with people, and yet be so terrible at managing their time. I think the answer is that time is not tangible. You cannot feel it or touch it or change it. It is the same every day. It never grows or shrinks, never moves faster or slower. It is what it is, but you will never see it. As the saying goes, "Time flies."

Another reason lies in the 'busy bee' syndrome. Don't people just love to tell you how busy they are? You might ask, "How are you doing?" And they reply something like, "I've been going crazy lately" or "Things are nuts right now." These same people love to tell you how tired and beat they are.. For these people mismanaging time is nothing more than a self-fulfilling prophecy. They have to live up to their own idea of how crazy or tired they are, so creating order in their lives does not fit into their definition of success.

I remember asking one of these busy bees why she always seemed so crazy. Her response was that she always had so much to do and not enough time for it all. I thought about this response later, and I realized that it wasn't that the busy bee had more to do than I did; in fact, she actually had less to do. The problem was that she was always focused on *everything* she had to do, instead of on the *next thing* she had to do. When you focus on everything, you become a lot less efficient and do a less-satisfactory job. When you focus on the next thing, you get that thing done more quickly and you do a better job of it.

To me, the idea of time not changing is encouraging. Time is not like the latest computer operating system. Just when you feel you have learned it, a newer version is released, leaving your current knowledge obsolete. Time, when managed correctly, can become one of your greatest tools in achieving success and living a fulfilled and happy life.

The Seven Rules of Time Management

I am sure that many of you have read the books that give you the seven steps to this or the seven principles for achieving that. Many of these steps and principles are very effective when you apply them, so I've decided to give you my seven rules of time management. I guarantee that, if you follow them, your life will flow a lot more easily

> *Let's get out of the habit of ignoring time and start respecting and mastering it.*

and you will be able to get a lot more done in a much shorter amount of time. Managing time is a skill, just like negotiating, singing, or playing a sport. It has to be practiced, and there are things you can do to make yourself better at it. Let's get out of the habit of ignoring time and start respecting and mastering it.

You have the same amount of time as everyone else, so why do some people always seem to have so much more than anyone else? Why do some people accomplish so much more in the same period of time? This chapter will help you become one of 'those people.' Nothing and no one is holding you back but yourself.

Rule 1: Learn to Use and Appreciate Technology

If you have never learned how to use a computer, listen up now! In our history, we have never seen so many inventions that have the ability to do so much good, but can also do so much harm at the same time. Technology can be a double-edged sword.

Take the *Blackberry*, for example. I don't think there's a device on the market today that can save you so much time. Recently, when I was getting the oil changed in my car, I got an offer for one of my real estate listings. The offer was scanned to my email, which came right through to my Blackberry. I forwarded the offer to the seller's email and called him, with my Blackberry, to go over the offer that was just coming into his computer. The offer was outstanding, and we decided to accept it without even making a counteroffer. My client printed out the offer, signed and dated it, and faxed it back to my e-fax, which goes directly into my email. I then forwarded the document to the buyer's agent for the buyer to sign, and had the agent scan it back to me. Deal done, and I never left the seat in the waiting room. It all took about 40 minutes. How do you like that? I went in for an oil change and while waiting made about $10,000.

In the past, I would have had to ask the agent to drop the offer at my office, drive the offer over to my client to review it, drive the offer to the agent's office, wait for the agent to have the buyers sign the offer, drive back to my office to make copies, and finally bring the original, signed document to the seller's attorney's office. Whew! What used to take at least a couple of days or more can now be done in a little more than half-an-hour, if you have the right tools. This is an example of how not wanting to adopt the new technologies can really cost you valuable time and, in the end, revenue. Why would someone continue to hire you for a particular job, when there are so many others who can do the same job in a fraction of the time?

There is another side to the Blackberry. Some people are becoming addicted to their Blackberries and can't stop looking at theirs to see if the red light is flashing. If you have the right mindset, though, and use Blackberries for their real purpose, you'll find them true professional time savers.

Another essential tool is *Bluetooth technology*. This technology allows you to speak on your cell phone hands-free, with either an earpiece or a connection in your car to your telephone that allows you to talk over the speakers. I have saved countless hours with this technology. Rather than staying late in my office, I can now call people on the way home. My car time, which used to be music time or dead time, is now call time.

Part of managing your time is learning to *spend the greatest amount of your work hours actually working*. Many people will say that they worked for 10 hours, when they really only worked for seven. Three hours were spent on Facebook, or searching on the Internet, or talking with friends, or shopping online. Use your work hours to actually work, and you won't have to keep working when you get home. That is the busy bee syndrome, and it's not fair to your family or to yourself. Some people love to tell you that they worked from sun-up to sun-down. Only a fool actually does this. Successful men and women work when they are supposed to work and spend time with family and friends when they are supposed to. True success requires this balance.

Email is another great time saver. I get over 200 emails a day from various clients, friends, and colleagues. Could you imagine trying to have that many telephone conversations each day, while trying to actually get other things done? The word 'impossible' comes to mind. The typical telephone conversation usually starts with some small talk, then turns to the subject of the call, and ends with formalities and more small talk. This can all take much more time than you need to give it.

Email allows you to get to a message you received at your convenience, but even more importantly, it allows you to write an answer or response to the sender without having time-consuming conversations. Because of this, I try to do as much communicating by email as possible. What could be a 20-minute phone conversation becomes a 15-second email.

Balance becomes important here, too. When you are growing or running a business, you never want to underestimate the power of human relationships. Nothing builds the foundation of a growing and lasting business like the relationships you have with others. There will be times, therefore, when you need to pick up the telephone and call the other person. Some things should not be left to email.

There are other downsides to email. It is easy for the tone of your emails to sound more negative than you meant. You must also make sure that your emails are sent to your intended recipient, especially if important information is attached. I always require confirmation that my email has been received whenever I am sending anything of importance.

Today's businesspeople must also have a *contact management database*. I don't understand how any business could thrive, especially in difficult times, without staying in constant contact with its past clients and leads. For many years, the real estate motto has been, "Location, location, location." I suggest a similar motto for businesses: "Database, database, database."

You can use your database to create a distribution list for a monthly newsletter, which should contain information that will be interesting and valuable to your contacts about your business and your industry. Your contact management database software should allow you to simply and easily download your distribution list and set up a schedule for sending out your newsletter. Whenever your newsletter goes out, hundreds, or even thousands, of people get something of value from you. You are staying in front of your target market without lifting a finger. Before technology, you would have had to see your targets face-to-face or stuff envelopes and put stamps on them, activities that could take days out of your month. Now, you can have as much of an effect on your targets without investing a second of your day.

A simple, but very effective, tool I recommend you invest in is a *navigation device*. Being late to just one appointment backs up the rest of your day and, even worse, creates a bad impression on your client or target. Investing the few hundred dollars in a navigation device can help assure that you will never be late again because you got lost. To be fair, I'm one who has to press 'home' on my navigation system when I'm heading home. It's not easy to claim to be the 'local real estate expert' when you have two clients in your car and you're driving down every street in a neighborhood trying not to act lost. I had lived a directionally-dysfunctional life up until I got my navigation device. Take my advice and let one help you as well.

Another must for all business people is a *scanner*. I think the days of faxing documents back and forth will come to an end soon. How many times have you faxed a document and then found out that it was illegible, so you have to fax it again or even worse track down the original? With a scanner, you can send right to your recipient's email, and the document gets there looking as clear to them as it does to you. At the same time, the document is saved on your computer, so you have access to it at any time. This is handy if the document must be sent to several people. For example, when I have a fully-executed contract on a real estate deal, I send a copy to the buyer or seller I represent, the appraiser, the other agent, and the attorney for my client. Can you imagine faxing to that many people when you could simply scan the document and send it to everyone at once? This is a tremendous time saver.

Along the same lines, every successful business person should have an *e-fax*. These cost about $10.00 per month and are a true bargain in terms of time saved. In practical terms, even though you might use all of the devices I'm recommending, some of the people you communicate with may not. If one of these people faxes something over to you that you need to send to several people, you need to be able to handle it. With an e-fax, the faxed document will be delivered directly into your email. Problem solved. You can now save the document and email it out to others as needed. Additionally, most e-faxes allow you to fax documents from your computer to other people's fax machines.

I am not exaggerating when I tell you that my scanner and e-fax have completely changed my business. I still keep files in manila folders for recordkeeping purposes, but all of my files are also on my computer. This means that when a past client contacts me about a past deal, I can easily locate and access the pertinent documents off of my computer, and all the information I need is right in front of me.

The last form of technology I will recommend relates to your industry. *Every industry has new technology* to make your life easier. Find out what it is, and use it. I can remember working in the moving industry and watching others using archaic methods for evaluating and estimating moving costs for clients. They would use long paper checklists and estimate the size and weight of the objects and piles of boxes they saw so they could come up with a cost estimate. And then they had to use another form to write up the quote separately, and then write a letter and mail the documents to the potential customer. I thought there had to be a better way of doing this. I convinced the vice-president of the company to invest in a Palm Pilot that came installed with software specifically created for the moving industry and a portable printer that was compatible with the tool. I could check everything off, and let the software calculate the weight and the price. I could then print out the estimate on the spot, or email the estimate before I even left the house. Don't you think this looked more professional to the potential clients? Sometimes you don't have to invest the time that was invested in the past on job functions, if you use the best technology and techniques available. Why waste more time than you have to?

You really should be able to find some sort of time-saving technology for your business and industry, which will allow you to operate more efficiently and more quickly. For my real estate business, I use a product called MLS Pulse, which allows my buyers to sign up and enter and save their search criteria. In the past, I would have had to check the Multiple Listing Service every day, sometimes several times a day, to search for what my clients wanted. When I first started in real estate, I even had to pull up the 'hotsheets' (which showed new listings and prices) every half hour or so, to see if anything came up that matched the search criteria so I could be the first agent to show the property. I was a slave to the hotsheets and spent a lot of time imprisoned to my computer. With MLS Pulse, when houses that match their criteria come onto the market, the details are emailed to my clients within 10 minutes. If the clients are interested, they can reply to the email, and I will get a message in my Blackberry. Communication has become instantaneous. I promise you that, if you look hard enough, you'll find some time-saving technology in your own industry. Do yourself a favor, and find out what it is.

You probably noticed that I didn't list a computer, cell phone, or photocopier in the list above. I consider these non-negotiable if you are going to be in business. If you want to take your business further, use the tools listed above as a starting point. You will save yourself time and operate much more efficiently if you take advantage of them. To summarize, I recommend using at a minimum the following tools:

1. Blackberry, or similar device
2. Bluetooth capability
3. Email
4. Contact management database
5. Navigation device
6. Scanner
7. E-fax
8. Industry-specific time-saving technology

Rule 2: Have Systems in Place

How many times have you heard someone say that you don't have to reinvent the wheel? This is true, except when you are first starting your business or when you realize that your business is not being run efficiently. All entrepreneurs have to be able to step back and take a look at their businesses and at how things are being run. Then, they have to ask themselves whether there is a better way to do something.

When I started my real estate business, I was on the telephone with my clients most of the day, holding their hands and walking them through every step of the process. I did this over and over with each of my clients. Why? Because I had the time and I was creating trust with my clients. But if what I'm preaching today about managing time is true, I couldn't do this today. There are just simply too many clients and not enough time in the day.

My answer? Systems, systems, systems. Many people think that great ideas are essential for a successful business, but great ideas are not enough. If you really want to be successful from the start, you have to come up with systems, apply the systems, make sure your whole staff understands how the systems work, and stick with the systems consistently.

Given the number of people I deal with every day, it would not be possible to explain all the miniscule details of every transaction. The key is to make them feel as if I have. I have a system that communicates to my clients everything they need to know and should expect in the process. When I meet a new buyer, I enter their contact information into my database, they automatically receive my monthly newsletter, and my assistant automatically sends them a letter thanking them for choosing to work with me. The letter also outlines what the buyer should expect over the coming days, how to sign up with MLS Pulse, and how to get a pre-approval letter (and why this is important); it even reviews a checklist of what to expect when we start to look at houses and what happens when we put one under contract. With this letter, I have taken the contents of a conversation that would take many hours and turned it into an easy way to answer all of my buyer's questions without spending one minute doing it. Do you think this buyer is impressed when she gets this letter? Do you think this separates me from my competition?

I wrote the letter back when I had the time to do so, and I spend approximately one second signing it before it is sent out.

I have similar letters that are sent to sellers who ask me to perform a market analysis for then, sellers that list their homes with me, sellers that just got contracts on their houses, buyers that just put a house under contract, and buyers and sellers that just closed on their homes. This sounds like a lot of letters, but again, I can send each one out in just one second, because I put my systems into place.

The key is to have all of the letters written and on your computer so you can send them out quickly. If you don't have an assistant, you can send out the letters yourself—in three minutes. Don't become a busy bee and feel that you have to write a personal letter to each client to make it more genuine. If you do so, you will never have enough time in the day.

Don't become a busy bee and feel that you have to write a personal letter to each client to make it more genuine. If you do so, you will never have enough time in the day.

I recommend using a similar system to send out quarterly announcements or any other updates you do throughout the year to your database. You should have an online calendar to remind yourself when to send out each of these items. Aim for the same time each year. For example, I send out a letter explaining my referral program every spring, right before the summer market season starts. It takes me only 10 seconds to tell my assistant to send out the referral letter, which is saved in our computers.

I have another system for dealing with the new listings I put on the market. My assistant has a checklist of all the things she needs to do with a new listing. She puts the listing on both boards in Connecticut, makes flyers that are left at the seller's house, creates and mails out postcards, creates a virtual tour and uploads it to the Multiple Listing Service and other sites, and updates my website with the listing. All of this is done automatically.

Do you have systems for handling all the telephone calls that come in? Does your assistant give you a piece of paper that can get lost on your desk, or does he send you an email with the subject 'new message' with the date on it? This allows you to search your messages by subject 'new message' so they are all in front of you when you sit down to call everyone back.

I could go through the fifty or so systems I use every day, but I think you're getting the point. In any business, while the work can change from day to day, the overall functions stay relatively the same. Why would you treat these functions inconsistently or as new each time? Take a step back and think about how you can become more systematic in your approach. Figure out how many hours you want to work each day and what systems you will use to make that happen. Much of your success comes down to the image that you present. A chaotic, unorganized image is just as powerful as a well-organized, professional one. But one draws people toward you, and the other pushes people away.

Rule 3: Don't Waste Time

Here comes the 'busy bee' syndrome again. How often have you heard someone say that they have been working from sun-up to sun-down? How many times have you said this yourself? As I've said, the truth is that the majority of people do not actually work all the time.

I am convinced that the majority of people waste an extremely large amount of time while they are supposed to be working. It is not uncommon to see people in your office engaging in small talk for 15 minutes or more on a fairly regular basis. I'm not suggesting that you become anti-social, but you do want to be careful about taking part in too many water cooler conversations. Having good relations at work is crucial in your growth and success, but work is not a social hour. Treat work as work, without becoming the office anti-social jerk.

You also need to be careful about who you spend your time with. When I first started my real estate team, I hired a lot of new agents with good potential and coached and trained them. A by-product of this was that I got pretty close to these people and took a real interest in their lives. BEWARE! This can cost you a lot of time and energy. I found that, whenever I came to the office, one of these agents saw me and decided it was time to lie on the couch and let the problems flow. You can imagine how difficult this was when I had a stack of things to do and a family waiting at home. I realized I was letting people who weren't valuing my time, have it. Not everyone is worth your time. I know that sounds harsh but when you reach a certain level of success, people will naturally gravitate towards you and want to be around you. This can be great, because you get the ability to speak into their lives, but it can also be very draining. Learn to navigate between the two. Remember, you only have so much time in each day. Let others who haven't learned these principles waste their time doing unproductive activities and having unproductive conversations.

I have reached the point where I don't feel bad when getting someone around me back on the work track. You are not doing anyone any favors by allowing them to vent frustrations and problems every day. On the contrary, refocusing them teaches them what is appropriate and inappropriate in the workplace and teaches them a tough principle that will contribute to their long-term success. Being a leader means doing what is right for yourself and others whenever possible. Leaders tend to see the whole picture when making decisions and usually try to project how those decisions will affect everyone, in both the short- and long-terms. In this example, you are gaining more time in the short-term and may even be helping these individuals' long-term careers.

If you are the one on the couch, letting your problems flow, remember that this can be as time consuming for you as for the one listening to you. There is a time and a place for having someone listen to you, but work time is not it.

Similarly, you don't want to get into the habit of being the 'nice guy' who offers to do everything. I have seen many nice guys and gals in offices, offering assistance to others whenever they see a need. Many of these people haven't created their own job descriptions, so they don't know what they are really supposed to be doing every day. I do know what I should be concentrating on. If you do adopt the 'fill the need' mindset at work, you will find that many people will start to lean on you for assistance whenever they get busy. You need to realize that you are not the office assistant. You are building your own business.

Another tactic for managing time is to look at each event and ask yourself if there will be some sort of profit from this meeting or conversation. The profit may come from learning something in a conversation or gaining a new friend if you enjoy their company. Again, the right friendships can be profitable because of the happiness and enjoyment they bring to your personal life. And personal success contributes to business success, because you function more effectively when you feel good about yourself. For example, I play tennis every Saturday morning. From a tactical standpoint, it doesn't make sense to be away from my family every Saturday morning, unless I gain something from it, which I do. I invest my time and money, but in return I have great, enduring relationships with the three men I play with…and I get to exercise a bit, as well. This is a win-win for all involved.

Relationships require a certain investment from you, but the return can be great if the relationships (personal and business) are with the right people. You really should be spending the majority of your time with the clients that make you the most money. I'm not saying that you should treat your clients differently, depending on how much money you make from them. In fact, part of your success should come from making sure that your least-profitable clients get a strong, positive feeling and that you roll out a red carpet for them, too. But the majority of your time should be spent with the people that you profit the most from.

When I first started my real estate business, my first listing was a $130,000 condo (not an expensive condo in southern Connecticut). I treated that condo as if it were the Taj Mahal and worked every lead I had to get a good deal on the property. By the time the condo sold, I turned this one sale into eight different deals all worth more than $200,000. I probably made almost $50,000 in commissions because of the steps I took to sell this one small condo. I probably wouldn't do this now, but early on I had the time to work a small deal into many more larger deals. Now, my time is spent on larger properties on which I can make the same amount of money on two to four deals as I made on nine deals back then. Think about it: Which would you rather spend your time on? You are going to put the same amount of work into and perform the same duties for both small and large deals, but your return on your investment will be greater with the larger deals. Think about how this principle applies to what you do.

Lastly, make it a point to audit what you are doing constantly and make sure that you are 'majoring on the majors and not on the minors.' Many people spend their whole day, even their whole lives, worrying about every little thing that someone said about them or did to them. This is a complete waste of time. Learn to deal with the big problems that come up and deserve your attention. Some people become so addicted to conflict that they create it, even if it doesn't exist. This causes great stress and limits your ability to think and function at your maximum capacity.

> *Many people spend their whole day, even their whole lives, worrying about every little thing that someone said about them or did to them.*

When I first started to taste a little success, I naively believed that everyone would be happy for me, as I would have been for them. Boy, was I wrong. I started hearing that people who barely knew me were muttering about me and saying negative things. At first, I was very annoyed, even angry. I believe, though, that a pivotal moment in my life was realizing that I could make the decision to fly like an eagle above the fray and the critics, or I could make the decision to rumble with the skunks. I went with the former, and I'm a better man for it. I love it when the bishop in my church talks about lifting your eyes above what is going on and focusing on what is to come. When you are focused on everything around you and not on what is to come, you will find yourself in a constant struggle to win every battle that comes along. I prefer to keep my eyes lifted on what is to come and ultimately win the war.

Here's a newsflash: If you don't want to waste time, don't make mistakes. Obviously, we all make mistakes every day, but isn't it true that some of the mistakes could have easily been avoided? I remember when I was in high school and going to my church's youth group on Wednesday nights, having conversations with the youth leaders about the different things I was doing and wanted to do. I think I was a pretty good kid, but nobody is perfect, and they saw it as their personal mission to keep me on the right path. I remember vividly the conversations when they were telling me what not to do. I was so curious, though, and I felt I had to have the opportunities to make my own mistakes so I could learn from them myself. If I understood then what I understand now it really would have made the lives of these volunteers so much easier. Taking what someone else has learned, whether from mistakes or from life in general, and applying it to your own life can save you an abundance of time and heartache, now and in the future.

I love how someone recently put it. He said that we need to constantly download information from great people and make their life lessons our own. We were talking about all of the books we had read over the years. I am particularly interested in business books, self-help books, and especially biographies. Biographies are usually written about extraordinary men and women who have accomplished great things, and they usually include life lessons. These books can teach you what it has taken these extraordinary people forty or so years to learn, and they're on sale for $20.00. These books are an amazing resource and I recommend that you take advantage of their wisdom.

The main key to my achieving success in such a short amount of time is this: I'm a sponge. If I can absorb the wisdom and life lessons of some of the greatest people of all time in a week's worth of reading, why wouldn't I take advantage of that? You may not think that this will save you time in the immediate future, but it will. When you gain wisdom from others who are smarter and more accomplished than you, you will be amazed at how your daily routines change and become more efficient. By working smart, you will not have to make up for time lost due to mistakes that could have been avoided. You should also strive to take larger steps in your pursuit of success than others do, because you work smarter than they do and have made the decision to be someone who learns from others' mistakes.

Rule 4: Make Lists...Schedule Everything

Making lists and not wasting time go hand-in-hand. I encourage you to start every day (or the night before) spending two minutes to write down what you need to do that day. You will be amazed how much more productive this makes you. You can focus on the next item to get done, instead of becoming overwhelmed by the massive amounts of work you have to do.

A by-product of focusing on what needs to get done is that you will find yourself concentrating more on the task at hand. We waste a lot of time trying to be good at everything, instead of great at just one thing. "Jack of all trades, master of none" applies here. Focus on doing what you are doing to the best of your ability until it is completed. When you have completed that task, move on to the next. Have you ever had a conversation with someone who was thinking about something else? You might as well be talking to a wall or a tree. At least the tree wouldn't act as if it was listening. You find yourself repeating what you just said, wasting more and more of your time. Tasks work the same way. You end up spending more time one each task than you have to because you are trying to finish them all at once.

When I was a child, I was convinced that my mother had me solely so I would do chores around the house. I learned at an early age how to wash dishes, take out the garbage, and vacuum. I can remember vividly one night when I was about eight years old, my mother asking me to sweep the kitchen after we ate dinner. I was not in the mood to sweep. In my head, I asked my mother, "Why don't you sweep the kitchen?" Of course this was in my head, because even at the age of eight I was not completely stupid. Dinner came and went, and it was time for me to sweep.

If you are always 'on call' for your cell phone, you can never give your best to your work or your home.

I got the broom and proceeded to sway it back and forth in a sweeping motion, so it would look to my mother as if I was working hard. When I was done, I put the broom back and proceeded to sit on the sofa in front of the TV. Within five minutes, I heard my mother yell, "JARED! GET BACK IN HERE!" Oh boy, I thought, here we go. My mother gave me one of her legendary lectures about how doing a job 'half-butt' is as good as not doing the job at all. When all was said and done, I had to sweep again and call for a new inspection. It took me almost half-an-hour to do a job that should have taken only two minutes. The lesson learned is to concentrate on the task at hand and do it right the first time; after all, doing half a job is as good as not doing the job at all. This lesson has stuck with me through the years.

If a list of tasks doesn't work for you, figure out what does. I don't make a list on a piece of paper or in a word processing program, but rather in a calendar program on my home page. I find it easier to list everything I need to accomplish the next day right in my calendar. I write my list of tasks in the 5:00 a.m. time slot so I keep my real schedule clear, but I can go back to the calendar to see what is next on the agenda.

Make sure that your list includes everything; don't leave certain items to chance ("I will do ABC when I get a chance…"). Your calendar is not just for business events, holidays, and birthday parties. It is for whatever you want to spend your time doing. If you think you are going to eventually pursue your passion for writing poetry, schedule a certain amount of time each day to do so. I love to spend time with my family. Would you believe that I actually put this on my calendar? Some might consider this callous or cold, but I have quality time with the wife and kids every day, while many of my critics try to fit it in when they get a chance. Don't let this be you.

Make sure that you are working the same time every day, if possible. This is especially important if you are self-employed and making your own schedule. If you are still in pajamas at 9:00 a.m. every morning, you are probably abusing your schedule flexibility. If you are always 'on call' for your cell phone, you can never give your best to your work or your home. Decide up front what your working hours will be and keep to your schedule. There is a reason why corporations make their workers come in and leave at the same time every day. Productivity is higher when workers know when they are working and when they are not.

Working long or strange hours should be the exception, not the rule. I watch many of my real estate co-workers working every day, night, and weekend, and they make a fraction of the money I make. They often work these crazy hours because their clients ask for it. But think about it. Does your doctor and dentist work around your schedule, or do you go on your lunch hour or take time off to see them? Usually, you are the one changing your schedule to accommodate them because they have other obligations and their time is valuable. Are you different? Do you have a family that wants you home? Is your time valuable?

Before I give a weekend or evening to clients, I ask myself:

Do they need odd hours, or could they make it during regular hours?

Are they worth it?

Do they appreciate that I'm working abnormal hours?

If the answer to any one of these questions is "no," they don't get my valuable time. I value my time that much, and so should you. When you start to value your time, others will value your time, as well.

One way you can tell whether someone values your time is if they are always late when they are supposed to meet with you. Don't let this happen. Once is permissible, but if you see a pattern, you need to address it. Why is it that some people always arrive a consistent 10-15 minutes late? They are able to keep a schedule, but it is their own disorganized schedule. This demonstrates a lack of respect for your time and should not be tolerated. The result of one late meeting is that you will show up late for your next meeting, have to apologize, and find that you are blamed. It is not worth it. Disorganized people are not worth your time.

Rule 5: Keep Your Schedule Flexible...Allow for Change

I see successful and almost-successful people make this mistake all the time: Because so many people want to talk with them, they set appointments with everyone. Remember Rule 3? Don't waste time with people who don't deserve it. Your head would spin if I told you how many mortgage brokers wanted to have lunch or meet me for coffee. The bottom line is that you can't spend your day booking meeting after meeting with

Always be cautious about forming business relationships with people who will benefit more from you than you will benefit from them.

people who, for the most part, are not going to contribute to your success. Success is a two-way street. Always be cautious about forming business relationships with people who will benefit more from you than you will benefit from them. The benefit should be roughly equal for you to spend your time.

I recently met with a person who wanted to show me his calendar for the coming week. Pride was oozing from his face, even though he was complaining about job stress. When I looked at his full schedule, all I could think about was how little time this person had to build for success.

Many success stories come from chance meetings. Last year, I was asked to appear on the A&E hit show *Flip This House*. This was a great opportunity that could boost my credibility and open many doors. The only issue was that they needed me in the next half-hour. The too-busy-for-business person would probably have missed the call, and even if he had taken it, he would have had to refuse, due to his full schedule. Because I had flexibility in my schedule, I was able to tell the producers I would be there in 20 minutes.

In business, unexpected things – good and bad – pop up all the time. Not allowing for the unexpected is planning for disaster. I don't know any successful businessperson whose days run exactly as planned. Opportunities come when least expected, and you don't want to be too busy to recognize them when they do. Part of success is capitalizing when your big break comes. Be ready for it!

Rule 6: Learn to Multitask and Create Shortcuts

You might think that multitasking conflicts with what I wrote earlier about concentrating on one task at a time, but it doesn't. Earlier today, I was on a conference call, and about half-way through I decided it was bland, so I started to do other things, as well. I checked emails on my Blackberry, while listening to a speaker ramble on and on. Although what she was saying was important, I could follow easily and even anticipate where she was headed. I was not concentrating on the task at hand; I couldn't fully pay attention to either the speaker or my emails.

When I recommend multitasking, I don't mean trying to do several important things at once. But many things do not require full concentration. Remember the example about how I put together a deal while getting an oil change? I did not need to watch the technicians drain my old oil, replace the filters, and put the new oil in. So I decided to use this free time to get other work done, which I then wouldn't have to bring home. I was multitasking by getting my oil changed and putting a deal together at the same time.

You would be really surprised if you spent a week documenting how much time you wasted that could have been productive time. Think about how much time you spend talking to co-workers, waiting on hold, day dreaming, getting coffee, driving to-and-from lunch, surfing the Internet, making personal phone calls, and so on. Instead, if you are driving someplace, return phone calls then. While you are waiting for a fax to come in, don't stand by the fax machine; instead answer some emails or write a document. This is the definition of multitasking: Doing multiple tasks at the same time. Start to recognize when you are just standing around, and start using the time to do something productive. Remember, every moment you spend just standing around is one less moment you get to spend with your family. When you train yourself to look at your schedule this way, you'll find that you change the way you spend your time.

Many of you will say that you do this all the time already. But, are you doing it intentionally? Yes, you may receive a phone call from a colleague when you are getting an oil change, but why don't you plan to make some calls yourself instead of just being available to someone else's call? Look for these opportunities throughout the day and week ahead, and plan on bringing work-related tasks with you. If you wait for ten minutes until someone calls you, you have wasted ten minutes you could have used to get something done and to get home ten minutes earlier.

Many times, we spend much more time doing certain activities than we need to. My policy is to play the fool only once, if possible. Try to find shortcuts in everything you do. Not shortcuts that make you do a bad or incomplete job, but shortcuts that allow you to work smarter and save you time.

In real estate now, the big craze is short sales. These happen when a seller is in pre-foreclosure and owes more on the house than it is worth; the lender on the house agrees to take less for the house than is currently owed. The process for a short sale is extremely time-consuming, because you have to call the lender whenever you need to talk with them, wait on hold for 30 minutes, and are then passed along to a different department. This can be very frustrating. I decided I could bypass this trouble by just getting the email address for the negotiator handing the case. Of course, the lender did not want to give me the address, but instead of giving up, I tried something else. The next time I was on the phone with a negotiator, I called from my car (that is, I was on the road). I was very pleasant and got the information I needed from the negotiator, and then I told her that I needed her phone number in case I had questions, but since I was on the road and couldn't write anything down, could she email me her contact information? She never would have given me her email address if I simply asked for it, but because she was willing to email me her contact info, I would now have her email address. Having her email address meant that I could get hold of her in two seconds whenever I needed her, rather than waiting for the hour I was used to when dealing with her bank. This is what I mean by a shortcut. Use your mind to figure out how you can create your own shortcuts and save time during your day.

Rule 7: Delegate

Learning to delegate was probably – and still is – the most difficult principle for me to learn. If you are a bit of a perfectionist and know exactly how you want things done, you will find it very difficult to delegate even the smallest of tasks to another person and trust that it will be done just as you would have. Think about it: Who cares more about your business than you do? The answer will always be "No one," because nobody cares more about your business than you do, nor should they. But you do have to learn to delegate at least some tasks to other people for the overall health of your business.

There is a time when it is appropriate for you to do everything for your business – when you have time to do it. Like any good business, though, yours is going to grow, and one person can handle only so much and continue to deliver the quality of services or products you want to deliver. If you hold on to the one-person mentality, you limit your business's ability to grow and, even worse, you use all of your time to do it.

> *Doing administrative tasks will only leave you feeling that you never have enough time in the day, but always have more to do.*

Nothing annoys me more than delegating a task to my assistant or an employee and finding that the result is incorrect or of insufficient quality. From a time-management perspective, I now have to spend even more time fixing the situation than I would have spent if I handled the whole thing myself. It becomes tempting to stop delegating, but that cannot be your answer. You have to use such situations as opportunities to show your people what they did wrong and to train them how to produce what you expect in the future. Spending this time now will save you countless hours in the future, because you will be able to delegate successfully. This is an investment of your time that you can expect a return on. You know the work will be done almost as well as if you did it yourself, which frees you up to handle other tasks that will bring in greater income or rewards.

Here is another way to think about delegating: Divide how much you make in an average week by how many hours you work. This will give you your average hourly wage. Use this number as a measuring stick to determine what tasks you should handle and what tasks should be delegated. If you make $100,000 per year, or $2,000 per week, and work about 40 hours per week, your average hourly rate is $50. The next time you are sending out a mailing, printing out postcards, or picking up paperwork from a client, ask yourself, "Is this a $50-per-hour job?", or more importantly, "Would I pay someone $50 per hour to do this?" If the answer to either question is "no," you should think about delegating the task from now on.

If you truly want your business to grow you need to focus on the tasks that an executive should be handling, such as meeting with clients or networking with others to build your professional brand. Doing administrative tasks will only leave you feeling that you never have enough time in the day, but always have more to do. Delegating (or hiring someone) will not only allow you to get more done, but will also reduce your stress and increase your level of energy. Your mind will be freed up, and you will find it easier to generate the ideas that will help you grow your business even more.

Still not convinced? For years, I wasn't either. I can remember other top professionals in my field saying over and over that you will never get to the top without an assistant. I can remember just as clearly thinking, almost arrogantly, "Well, you are not me; I can do it." For years, I hired assistants and fired them shortly afterwards, even though they were doing a great job, because I didn't think I was justified in paying them what I was. It was my fault. I come from a very thrifty background, and even if I become a billionaire some day, I will probably always compare prices for everything I buy to determine if I really need it.

Finally, in 2008, I decided that I was going to bring someone in and give it a real try. At first, it was tiring, because I had to train my assistant in all of my systems, and give her all of my passwords; worse yet, I was accountable to her. The funny thing is, when you hire someone and show her your systems, she actually expects you to follow them! I found out that, because of my busy schedule, I was unintentionally bypassing many of the systems I had set up without realizing it. The results were unbelievable. I don't think I have to tell you about the real estate market in 2008; activity in my local market dropped 32%. Regardless, thanks to my new assistant and the accountability she forced, my personal business increased 70% in 2008. Was the small investment I made in my assistant worth it? I am home for dinner 95% of the time, don't work too many weekends, and get to spend as much time with my wife and children as I choose to.

Working everything into your schedule is not always easy, but the truth is that you make time for the things that you want to. I am not home for dinner every night because I don't have other things that I could be doing. I am home for dinner because I make it a point to be and I put my family first. Sometimes, I leave the office knowing that I could have stayed there all night handling file after file, but I know that I want my children to look back and remember that, no matter how busy daddy was, dinner time with them was more important. I can't tell you how many nights I have stayed up into the early morning hours, after my wife and children have gone to sleep, finishing the work that I could have been doing earlier that evening. Working late like this shouldn't happen that often if you manage your time wisely, but when it does, remember who comes first and why.

Chapter 7

Developing the Right Mindset

Success is a mindset. I saw an interview with Donald Trump once where he said that making the first billion dollars was tough, but once he did it, he no longer worried about making money or even losing what he had already made because now he knew how to do it. I won't even try to compare my business success to what The Donald has achieved, but I do kind of know what he means.

When I was younger than I am now, I was completely driven to be successful. I wanted to run a successful business. I wanted to prove to myself and others that I was different and could do it. Now that I have achieved a certain level of success, I have a sense for what he was saying. I have seen the characteristics of successful people. I have seen the decision making process of successful people. I have built my career in real estate from the ground up, and even if it were all taken away tomorrow, I would still know how to do it all over again. These principles don't just apply to my field of business. Every path I have come across in my life I have seen the same successful patterns at work. Whether it was working full-time in high school, selling knives in college, or working in the real estate business now. I have learned more as I have gone along, but it is not a mistake that I have been abnormally successful with every venture I have put my hands to.

Failures are tough to embrace, but you have to. I have read so many books that tell you to learn from your failures, because they are as big a part of your success as your achievements. I could not agree with this statement more, as long as you do not get comfortable with your failures and use them as a crutch. There is no doubt that I have experienced plenty of failure in my life, but it is the hatred and almost fear of that failure that I use to motivate me. I know 'fear' is a strong word and not one I usually like to use, but it is the best way that I can describe it. It is not that I am afraid of failing when I start something new, because I have played it out in my head and given it great thought. But rather, it is the idea of dedicating so much time to succeeding at something, only to have it blow up in my face and be a complete waste of time. This fear of failure should motivate you, as well. I don't do anything unless I truly believe that it will be a wild success. Understand what I just said: Not a 'success,' but a 'wild success.' There is not enough time in the day or in our lives to spend it doing mildly successful things. Mild success is common. Wild success is less common and harder to achieve, but the rewards are greater. This is the mindset that you have to have if you are going to achieve a different level of success. Some people are satisfied with blending in at a certain level of success, and that is okay for them. But this goes back to the idea of knowing who you are, and I am fully aware that that is not me.

Chapter 8

Developing Traits for Success

I have found that successful people tend to be successful for very specific reasons. People do not become successful accidentally – even a lottery winner had to buy a ticket in order to win. I have tried to study successful people by reading their books, spending time with them, or following them from a distance on television, in interviews or in similar situations. I have come up with 10 traits that I have either noticed in the majority of these successful people, or believe that you should develop if you are going to become successful.

Trait 1. Practice Action

If you were born in the last 100 years, you have probably seen the movie *Top Gun*. This movie starred Tom Cruise in his younger days and told the story of a few brash fighter pilots who trained in a Navy program known as Top Gun. This was THE movie of its time, and I idolized Tom Cruise's character as a kid. There is one line that stands out from that movie to this day, when the characters Maverick and Goose emphatically stated, "I feel the need, the need for speed!" Who knew how prophetic these words would become?

From a success prospective, these words are crucial. About five years ago, an agency polled the top 100 companies in the world and asked them to name one thing to which they attributed the success of their company. The agency was expecting to hear things like customer service, accountability, technology, or good management. These answers came up occasionally, but do you know what the number one answer was? It was something known as *speed of implementation.*

Very simply, speed of implementation means that when you hear a good idea, you implement it immediately. You take action. Have you ever gone to a conference and listened to great speakers and presentations and left thoroughly charged up, only to go home and do exactly what you have always done? I know I have. I like to think of this as taking part in a 'shelf-help' conference. The information that was meant to help you better yourself ends up just sitting on the shelf somewhere. But when you decide to implement good ideas at the moment that you learn them, things begin to change.

For the longest time, managers, CEOs, and leaders from all walks of life believed that whoever has the most and best ideas, wins. They would have brainstorming sessions, trying to come up with idea after idea that they knew would help them break through to a different level. These brainstorming sessions were very valid

> *Great ideas are nice, but they are nothing without action.*

and may still be useful today. But there is something even more important than good ideas, and that is the *speed at which you implement good ideas.*

Recently, I was going over some notes that I had taken at real estate conferences over the last few years and I saw a multitude of great ideas. To me, this proved my point even more. Great ideas are nice, but they are nothing without action. It is like the saying that "Knowledge is power." No it's not. Knowledge *when applied* is power. The real power in anything you do always lies in the doing, the action you put behind it.

What I tend to see in one successful person after another is not just their ability to come up with great ideas, but their drive to take action. If you are reading this book and have become motivated to start a business or do anything productive, don't waste this opportunity. Act! Don't stop at the dreaming stage. The dreaming stage is important but nobody is going to pull your dream out of your head. It is your responsibility to bring it through to fruition. No one is going to do it for you.

Similarly, if you are already in a business and have some great ideas to propel you forward, try it! You miss 100% of the shots you don't take. If no one is going to get hurt in the process, why wouldn't you take action? Your success depends on it.

Trait 2. Know How to Communicate

Successful people are able to communicate. Remember how Ronald Reagan was called 'The Great Communicator?' This is what you should aspire to be.

To understand communication, you have to understand what it is not. Most people initially think that communication is speech or verbal. According to A. Barbour, author of *Louder Than Words: Nonverbal Communication*, words only make up 7% of communication. An additional 38% of communication is vocal, or your volume, pitch, and rhythm. And 55% is body language, including your facial expressions and how you move your hands, shoulders, and every other part of your body. You would be wise to note that the words you use are actually the least important part of your communication process. In other words, it is not what you say, but how you say it.

Sometimes, it doesn't matter how you say something; the result will be the same. Have you ever asked a woman when she is due, only to find out that she is not pregnant? Ouch! No amount of joking or smooth talking can get you out of this situation. Ask me how I know? The one time I did ask this question to the wrong person, I experienced awkwardness like you have never dreamed of. I heard crickets making noises in every which direction. It was bad. I followed up by saying that, "I thought I had heard that she was pregnant and I was confused because she certainly didn't look pregnant." That is about as good as you can do under the circumstances.

You do have to be mindful of what you say. Just as you value yourself, you also have to value what you say. As I said earlier, I really used to just talk and talk and give my opinion about everything. Over time, I learned that doing this made others consider my opinion less valuable. I am able now to say more and be more effective with fewer words. Learn to speak with confidence, and, more importantly, learn to speak when invited to speak, and you will have learned a lesson that many people take their whole lives to figure out. It is not about the quantity of what you say. It is about the quality of what you say. The quality of what you have to say increases and carries more weight if your audience asks for your opinion and knows that you think before you speak.

Don't ever talk down to other people. Part of being successful is being a leader, which means that you'll need people to follow you. Most people do not want to follow leaders that they don't feel safe around, who belittle others to build themselves up. On the contrary, use your communication skills to build others, and you will be amazed at how quickly people line up to follow you. There is a way to present yourself and use your body language and tone in a way that projects success and leadership, without feeling that you have to prove that you are the captain of the room. When I hear people blowing their own horns too much and making sure that you know who they are and what they have accomplished, it actually has the opposite effect on me. Their words mean nothing to me, because I know that the people who are loud and trying to portray themselves as lions are usually the ones who are most afraid and, under it all, most like lambs.

When you realize that words are only 7% of communication, you can finally realize that talking away won't do that much for you. Carrying yourself in a confident manner can take you a lot further. Nor it is about telling everyone your accomplishments. In fact, I have found that when you carry yourself a certain way, over time people begin to ask you questions and dig further to know more about you. They will actually respect you even more when they find out what you have accomplished. They know that they would have been telling everyone about their accomplishments, and they appreciate that you are different. Yes, you may have a select group of people you share accomplishments with, but how you carry yourself and what you *don't* say have to become part of how you communicate.

You also have to learn to control your volume, pitch, and rhythm. I don't trust people who are always ecstatic or who lose their cool very easy. You want to communicate a certain level of calm with everyone you come in contact with and not make dramatic emotional responses too frequently in front of people. Some of you may have to practice controlling yourselves more than others.

We cannot forget the words, even though they are the least part of the communication process. Almost daily, I see people use the wrong words and tone in situations. I just overheard a conversation in which two real estate agents were negotiating, and the seller's agent just shouted at the buyers' agent, "Well, do they want my seller's kids thrown in the deal as well!" This agent believed that the buyers were being unreasonable in their requests and this was her way of letting the buyers' agent understand how she felt. From a communication point of view, this was not the way to handle the situation. A better way would have been to understand why the buyers were requesting everything they were and to realize that they were nervous and needed some extras thrown in to demonstrate to themselves that they were getting a good deal. A better response from the seller's agent would have been something like, "My seller is going to be flattered that they like her furniture so much and think it goes so well with the style of the home that they want it. I know my seller has worked hard over the last twenty years to maintain and decorate her house to keep it looking as beautiful as possible. I will present this to her and see what she says, but I will tell you that she is selling her home for $20,000 less than the last home in this neighborhood sold for and she will probably need her furniture in her new house. At minimum, I think I may be able to get the seller to leave her lawnmower and patio furniture, but I will check." Saying something like this doesn't raise the other agent's defenses, but more importantly it reaffirms that the seller has meticulously maintained the home and that the buyers are getting a good deal. It also does give the buyers something – the lawnmower and patio set – so they will feel that they have gotten something in return. Furthermore, this reminds the buyers that the seller is buying a home, too, which will reassure them about their own purchase. Do you see the difference? One response started an argument or planted the seeds of ill will, while the other addressed the underlying reasons for the buyers' request and reassured them about their purchase. You really have to understand your audience when communicating.

This leads to the next point: Communicating is listening. You have two ears and one mouth. Just as in the example above, if you are not listening so you can hear what really needs to be communicated, you won't know what your message must be. We frequently just give answers and rebuttals, without listening to what the other person has truly said. I have been guilty of this on more than one occasion.... today. Make it a point to take a whole day and actually listen to what other people say. You really should not plan how you are going to respond to others before they even finish what they are saying. When you have a mind that works quickly, you are more likely to fall into this trap than others.

Learning to listen to others will not only benefit you in a conversation, but it can also become your ultimate weapon when negotiating. Most people when negotiating will tell you what they are really looking for, without directly saying it.

They will make little comments that allude to what they really want. For example: An agent is trying to negotiate a deal with me for my listing, gives me her client's offer, and goes over the terms; I will usually say, "Thanks so much; I will see what I can do." That should be the end of the conversation, but every once in a while an agent says more, like "Yeah, so uh, just see if you can get me something. Just tell your sellers this is a starting offer." When an agent says this, she is basically telling me that her buyers are starting with a low offer, but they are more than willing to raise the offer, if needed. I know at this point to come back with a high counteroffer and stand firm to get my sellers the most money possible for their house. Many people would have rushed off to phone their clients and not paid any attention to this very important final line from the other agent.

You might be asking yourself what this has to do with success or how this will make you money. Remember that success is more than money, and truly successful people tend to have great relationships which depend on their ability to communicate. That is true whether you are talking to your spouse, best friend, business associate, or whomever. Some of the greatest lifelong contacts, whether personal or business, will come about solely because of your ability to communicate. The impression that you make on someone in the first sixty seconds could make the difference between them becoming an ally for the next thirty years or writing you off as someone that they don't want to be associated with.

Trait 3. Know Your Strengths and Weaknesses

Knowing your strengths and weaknesses will help you avoid a lot of missteps in your life. Many bad decisions are made by people who think they are great at everything. Truly successful people know that this is not so. You can find out what your strengths and weaknesses are just by listening to the people around you.

We all know people who are living out there on their own little flying saucers under the motto, "I don't care what anyone else thinks about me." If you don't know people like this, you probably are one of them – a little food for thought. These types of people will tell you that all that matters to them is what they think about themselves. You couldn't find more manure in a cow pasture. The truth is these people usually care about what others think about them far more than the average person does. They have simply been hurt by what others have said about them for years and feel as if they have to create this defensive barrier around them to protect themselves. This is extreme behavior. I understand it, but I don't advise it.

If you are an authentic and genuine person, you really should care what others think about you. Many of your critics see your every decision. They watch as you go through your ups and downs, and many of them even care about the outcome of your decisions. Not everyone around you has the same degree of influence over you, but just because someone disagrees with you, doesn't mean they need to be excommunicated from your decision making process. Many times you will find that there is a measure of truth in just about everything that others say about you or to you. This can be tough to swallow when you think about some of the things people have said about you. It can either depress you or make you stronger. I have chosen the latter. When others try to bring you down to their level, you can choose to accept what they are saying and limp back into your corner, or you can find the speck of truth in what they are saying and begin to make some changes. This is the genesis of realizing what some of your weaknesses are.

As a younger adult, I was often considered cocky and arrogant. I had the world at my fingertips, and I knew it. I was making good money at the time, had a good personality, was relatively athletic, and was fairly popular with the ladies. I knew that many of the people closest to me looked up to me, and I really let it get to my head. I started thinking that I was better than I was. It wasn't long before I was hearing rumors from friends about things that others, I wasn't close to, were saying about me. These very same critics saw me every week and couldn't have been more pleasant to me face-to-face. At first, I was angry and ready to confront these people. How could they say these things about me? I was never anything but nice to them. Who are they to talk about me behind my back? Then it dawned on me that maybe what they were saying was right. Maybe I had gotten a little too big for my britches. My friends either didn't want to say it or didn't see it in me because they didn't want to. In the end, I wasn't bothered enough to confront my critics, but I did decide to learn from them. The lesson I learned was that, no matter how big or important or great you think you are, you are really only as big, important, and great as the people around you. Those closest to you know who you really are. Cherish your relationships with these people, because if you decide to put the lessons in this book into practice, chances are you will become successful. You will make a lot of money and you will have a great family life. But even more important, you will need people around you who don't let your success go to your head. Almost every gift we have comes as a double-edged sword. If you are usually a very happy person, you may be susceptible to swings of depression, as well. Similarly, people who have great financial abilities and intellect have to be careful not to become too arrogant and proud.

Another of my weaknesses could best be described as anti-social-ism. That is probably putting it mildly. Many people can't wait for the next picnic or lunch gathering or meetings with friends. I am happy for these people, but I can't say I am a card-carrying member of their club. My father and I like to joke that God gave the two of us the skills to socialize, but we only use them when we are backed into a corner.

You can see why this would be a weakness for someone working in an industry that requires going to social events, talking to lots of people, and networking on a regular basis. I had to make a decision to either learn to overcome this weakness or try to become the first real estate agent on the face of the earth who did a lot of business without ever approaching anybody. What decision would you have made? Me too. I decided to stretch myself a little bit and make more of an effort to be friendly and socialize, even when I didn't have to. I started setting up lunches with people and talking with them. I sent little notes to people about what was going on in the market. I joined my local Chamber of Commerce and started to attend a weekly leads group meeting, eventually becoming the co-chair. I went to picnics frequently and even held gatherings at my own house. I was a new man. This never would have happened if I hadn't realized that one of my weaknesses was going to be a huge impediment in the growth of my career.

If you are not sure what your weaknesses are, ask someone. If you are married, your spouse knows. Everyone has weaknesses, but not everyone identifies them and deals with them. If you do deal with your weaknesses, you will already be separating yourself from the pack and moving yourself closer to success. When it comes down to it, you shouldn't have to learn about your weaknesses when someone tells you in a heated argument. Find out for yourself what they are and work on them.

I had to understand and use my strengths, as well. I knew that I was good at administrative work, because I always liked things fully categorized and in order. I am a big advocate of having systems in my business, and you should be for your business, as well. Systems save you a ton of time and ultimately make you look more professional to your clients. I also knew that I was good at dealing with people, even if I didn't want to. It was time to unleash this skill and get in front of people.

My degree was in marketing management, and I felt I was pretty good at getting myself out in front of the public in cost-effective, but productive ways. I knew I was a hard worker, but I wanted to become a *smarter* worker. I knew that people had been drawn to me ever since I was kid. I never had trouble making friends and was usually the leader of our packs, almost by instinct. I would need this leadership ability to take me to the top of my craft. Lastly, I knew I had an advantage over many of my fellow realtors because, while I recognized one of my weaknesses was my youth, I also saw it as a great strength. While many of my colleagues resisted change and didn't want to discover many of the new ways of doing things, I grew up with the Internet, email, and other forms of technology that could take my business to the next level. Additionally, many of the buyers in the market for a house were first-time home buyers and would prefer to work with someone of similar age. My job was just to find ways to become visible. Buyers had to learn that I was available to work with them and that I was the best option.

Trait 4. Never Stop Learning

The main key to my success, or the success many others have achieved in a short amount of time, is: Become a sponge and never stop learning. If I can gain the wisdom and life lessons of some of the greatest people of all time in a week's worth of reading, why wouldn't I take advantage of that?

Successful people never stop learning. Recently, I was having a conversation with someone about good investments, and the person looked up at me and said, "Well, what am I going to tell you?" You can respond in one of two ways to this type of question. You can think, "I already know it all. What can you possibly teach me?" Or you can think, "I can learn something from just about everyone I talk with." I hope the first response is not the one that comes to mind. Notice that I said 'just about everyone,' not everyone. Some people just talk and talk and talk and nothing worthwhile ever comes out. For the most part, you should take the 'eat up the meat, spit out the bones' approach to your conversations. Nobody knows it all.

Besides picking up the typical street knowledge that successful people learn everyday, there are other ways to learn as well. One way is by reading books. If I told you how many books I have read about successful people or books about finances or politics, it would make your head spin. I am particularly interested in business books, self-help books, and especially biographies. Biographies are usually written about extraordinary men and women who

> *If I can gain the wisdom and life lessons of some of the greatest people of all time in a week's worth of reading, why wouldn't I take advantage of that?*

have accomplished great things, and they usually include life lessons that the person has learned. You can find in one book what it took these extraordinary people forty years or so to learn. And the book is on sale for only $20.00. This is an amazing resource to take advantage of!

One of the best ways to continually learn and grow is to find experts in your field who you trust and find out whether they have created any products for you to purchase. These products may include books, CDs, DVDs, and various kinds of communications. I find that I regularly listen to instructional CDs in my car and office. These CDs keep me motivated and give me new ideas. They are well worth the money I spend on them. In fact, when you realize how much additional money you can make from this type of learning, you'll realize that these products are an absolute bargain, if not a steal.

Many business books say the same things, but you can pick up one or two pearls of wisdom, make them your own, and begin to apply them to your work. This can make the time you invested in reading worthwhile. I don't use the word 'invest' by accident. Successful people do look at the time they spend reading as an investment because, ultimately, they expect a return on this investment. So should you.

You should constantly be learning about your field or industry or about the work you want to do. Read industry magazines, find websites that provide useful information, and associate with people you can learn from. I find that I prefer to mingle with people who have more, or at least similar, knowledge about the topics that interest me so we can be like 'iron sharpening iron' and grow through each other. When you stop growing, you are either dead or close to it. And that's not a good place to be.

In addition to self-teaching, there is something to be said for the formal education, as well. Many successful people have gone back to school to get their MBAs, or even just to finish the schooling they started many years ago. When I started in real estate, I was going to school at night to complete my degree, and to this day, it is one of my proudest accomplishments. I said for years that my degree in marketing would never do anything for me, because I didn't need a degree to be in real estate, and I was wrong. Yes, you don't need a degree in marketing to be in real estate, but it sure does help to be an expert in marketing. I use what I learned in my courses every day. I hear stories all of the time about people who have succeeded without going to college or even finishing high school. Yes, you can succeed without an education, but the path is more difficult.

Education is a life-long process and can come in many different forms. Successful people take advantage of whatever form of education is available to them, not only for their current success, but to prepare for their future success. You never know what the most unexpected person or article will teach you, so keep an open mind. Nobody knows everything.

Trait 5. Live a Healthy Lifestyle

Real success involves your body, as well as your mind. I can't tell you that the majority of successful people live a healthy lifestyle, because many that I have come into contact with do not. I am writing about the exceptions that do.

Picture yourself as an automobile. When you reach a certain level of success in your life you become like a Mercedes Benz. You look great on the outside and purr like a kitten, but if you don't maintain yourself, you will have a minimal shelf life ahead of you. The natural by-product of success is having so many people and options pulling you in so many different directions that it can become tiring. Truly successful people understand this and counteract it by making an effort to live healthy lifestyles.

A healthy lifestyle means that you don't eat fast food for lunch everyday. It may be more difficult to bring lunch from home or to go to a healthier restaurant, but your health deserves it. Like everything else, this is about balance. There may be times when you have to use the drive-thru lane of your local fast food place, but don't make a habit of it. If you are someone that knows the numbers of your favorite value meals at every fast food restaurant, listen to what I am saying here.

Another part of a healthy lifestyle is rest. You are no good to anyone if you are tired all the time. I have a very hectic schedule and run three different businesses. But I also have a two-year-old with limitless energy who doesn't want to hear that daddy is tired when I get home. And do you think my four-month-old son can be told to stop crying in the middle of the night or put himself back to sleep because daddy has had a rough day? I don't think so, but I still have to find time to rest. Remember the time management principle: Schedule everything. If you know ahead of time what your family expects from you, plan accordingly. Find a time each day for rest, whether first thing in the morning, in the middle of the afternoon, or before you go to bed. Rest is important if you are going to achieve anything in this life. Some of my greatest time-saving and money- saving ideas have come in my times of rest. Imagine yourself as a car needing a fill-up every now and again. No one can run on Empty for too long.

Trait 6. Practice Philanthropy and Don't Forget Where You Came From

According to Wikipedia, philanthropy is the act of donating money, goods, services, time and/or effort to support a socially-beneficial cause with a defined objective and with no financial or material reward to the donor. In other words, you are working for the benefit of another without pursuing any sort of gain for yourself.

I have always believed that you reap what you sow. We all know people who have done well for themselves and, to be quite honest, we don't understand why. On the other hand, we all know people who are wildly successful and we couldn't be happier for them because they seem to handle their success as we believe we would if we were more successful, right?

We all want to believe that if we made it big, we would help the less fortunate, donate money and time, and open an orphanage in Africa. This doesn't come naturally. To me, true philanthropy is about sacrifice. When a billionaire gives a charity one thousand dollars, he doesn't even know how to measure that thousand dollars. It means nothing to him in the larger scope of things. But when you or I give a thousand dollars, we notice that the money is gone, and we probably want to make sure it is used well, because we know what we could have done with it. We all want to make sure that whenever we give up something for someone else, it means something to us. For that billionaire, it may be more of a sacrifice to give up an hour of his time than to donate a thousand dollars.

You never want to get so focused on your own life that you forget that others out there don't have what you have, as little as it may be. I am very thankful that I got to experience a different way of life as a child and wasn't sheltered. I had the privilege of seeing firsthand the struggles that people go through and the anxieties that parents take on when they are trying to figure out how to get their child a new pair of shoes or put food on the table every day. Experiencing this made an indelible impression on me, and I will never forget what people go through and how hard it can be for them. If you haven't experienced struggles like this, thank God, but don't ignore what is going on around you. You just may be the answer to someone's prayer. That is a powerful concept if you think about it.

Few people have become successful without the helping hand of others. You should always try to make it a practice to remember those people in your life who have helped you along the way and never to forget where you have come from. Thinking like this allows you to develop the empathy needed to help others when they need it most because you never know when you will be the one who needs the help of another person.

Trait 7. Be Competitive

Being competitive in a healthy way can make up for a lot of your shortcomings. Even as a child, I seemed to be successful at almost everything I tried to do. That is not because I was so great, but it had more to do with my drive to succeed. I always wanted to be the best. If I was selling shoes and heard that someone from another store had sold more shoes than I did, I would ask for more hours and try to sell even more shoes. It didn't matter what I was doing; I always wanted to be the best.

There is no doubt that you can take competitiveness too far, and on more than one occasion, I have. But as I have matured and grown, I have learned how to harness my competitiveness and use it for my benefit.

When you look at some of the greatest athletes, business men, or achievers of our time, you almost always find competitiveness within them and it would serve you well to develop it, too. When you are competitive, you'll find that even if you're having a bad day and don't feel like working, dealing with people, or smiling, the fact that you don't like to lose can drive you through to the end of the day. Sometimes, this drive is all you have and many times it is all you need.

Trait 8. Love What You Do

Finding out what you love to do is half the battle of success. It ties into the idea of balance. You may be successful at something you don't love, but you won't be as successful. Even if you appear to be successful, if you are unhappy, you have only achieved a measure of success. Remember, success is more than just job achievements or deposits in your bank account. Wouldn't you love to want your children to follow in your footsteps because you want them to do what you do? You know it will make them as happy as you are.

When I was a teenager, I vividly remember an interesting conversation with my uncle. My uncle was a different type and I loved him to death. His wardrobe was ten pairs of exactly the same jeans and 10 shirts that were exactly the same. Every day, he wore the exact same thing, even though he changed his clothes. He smoked and drank heavily and spent a lot of time with me. He was not a sophisticated man and probably scared a lot of people when he walked by them. He did have that kind of a look. For over 20 years, he was the city mason, doing back-breaking work. When we hung out, he would try to share little pearls of wisdom that he had learned from his mistakes over the years. One pearl he shared with me stuck with me to this day. He said, "Jared, I work my tail off and literally build things brick by brick no matter what the temperature or weather happens to be. Everyday, I am supervised and told what to do by a man in a suit who is not working half as hard as I am, but is making

> *Remember, success is more than just job achievements or deposits in your bank account.*

twice as much. When you get older, do what he does, not what I do."

This was an amazing statement and it showed me that he did not love what he did. He simply had to do the job he did because of past mistakes he had made. He didn't have many other options. I am not putting down manual laborers; many people wearing suits wish they were out building houses. This is a call to wake up and do what you love to do whether that means starting a landscaping business or building websites. One is not better than the other, unless the person doing it actually loves what he or she does. Successful people don't feel the need to fit into everyone's idea of what is acceptable for them to be doing with their lives. They carry their own compasses and decide on their own paths, based on their own passions. It is not easy to do this, but the rewards are worth it.

Trait 9. Become an Overcomer

Many successful people are where they are today because they didn't stop moving forward the first time adversity hit. I hear all too often that, when you are doing what you are meant to be doing, doors will just open and opportunities will present themselves to you. While it is true that doors do occasionally open, it is unreasonable to believe that you will not face challenges as well. In fact, I would say that you may face even more trials when you are on the right path. It is during these trials that you will figure out if you are on the right path or not because the testing that comes with these challenges will determine whether your resolve is great enough to succeed.

How many people do you know who have been 100% committed to what they are doing, but move on to something new the next month? I know plenty of these people. Successful people, however, are overcomers. They not only are able to overcome challenges, but they anticipate them. While others are pointing to problems, they point to solutions. Your mindset has to be that of a good marriage. "No matter what comes my way, I/we will persevere."

If you are going to succeed, failure cannot be an option. When the winds of problems and issues come your way and knock down everything you have struggled to build, the successful person's reaction is to rebuild better and stronger, while the unsuccessful person starts to think about what else they can do. They say things like, "Well, I guess it just didn't work out. I gave it a good shot." Or my personal favorite, "It just wasn't meant to be." What they are really doing is using the trials as excuses for failure, because many of them are subconsciously afraid of success and the pressure that comes with it. That cannot be your mindset. Fear cannot be an option, either, and if it is, you have to conquer it. Success is the only option, no matter how hard it is to achieve and how elusive it may seem to be.

Trait 10. Do What Others Will Not Do

I am always amazed at people who want to reach the highest levels of success, but are not willing to put in the work necessary to get there. When I hear about someone who has become successful, I am more interested in their climb than I am in their current success. Their process intrigues me so much more because I learn more by seeing how they became successful than by seeing them already successful.

When I was in high school, I had a very prestigious job at a little place called K-Mart. My job was pretty much whatever needed to get done. At times I was at the register; at other times I was a 'stock boy;' and during certain seasons I worked in the florist wing or Christmas shop. Even at this young age, I watched my peers as they would try to find every way possible *not* to work. They would hide in parts of the store not covered by security cameras, or take extended breaks if the manager wasn't on top of them. Yes, occasionally, I came back from lunch late, but for the most part, I really did have a different attitude about everything. I showed up on time, and without knowing what I was doing, I did do the jobs that no one else wanted to do.

As a store employee, there is almost nothing you hate more than hearing over the intercom, "Clean-up on aisle 9, Clean-up on aisle 9. I need sales associate Jared to aisle 9." When you hear this, you know you are about to be humbled, while cleaning up after someone else with everyone watching. Sounds exciting right? Well, it actually sounds pretty good compared to what the intercom said one weekend.

It started out as a normal weekend. I was stocking shelves, minding my own business, and then it happened. The intercom came on and, almost in slow-motion speech, said the words, "Clean up in restroom one. I need sales associate (insert name) in restroom one." This went on for about 10 minutes with various names being inserted into the request. After a few other sales associates' names were called out over the intercom with no success, suddenly my name was called. Are you kidding me! That was my first response, only maybe in much different words. It was obvious that I was being called to do a job that many others had turned down over the past ten minutes. The only question was "Why?" I had no idea what I was going to see when I got into that bathroom. As I approached the scene of the crime, I saw people gathered around the restroom door. I expected to see a chalk outline of a body, but what I saw was even worse: watery and brown and mixed with what the other associates had left behind due to their light stomachs.

It wasn't easy, but I got the job done. To this day, that may have been the hardest job I have ever done. People usually say that you have to be willing to clean the toilets when they are talking about being willing to do what others are not, but I would gladly clean toilets with a toothbrush before I ever again have to clean up anything like what I cleaned up that day. My reward was a pat on the back from the store manager and a $10 gift card from K-Mart for my service. I can still remember the store manager looking me in the eye afterwards and saying, "If you can do that, you are going somewhere, kid." From that day on, that store manager looked at me differently and treated me differently. I got preferential treatment from him and even got a raise shortly thereafter. I had proven to him that I was willing to do what had to be done, even if I didn't directly benefit from it. I believed that doing what others weren't willing to do was going to pay off for me one way or another, and I was right. If you are honest with yourself, you know where you are taking shortcuts. You know where you could be working harder and smarter. Separate yourself from the crowd and show people that you are willing to do whatever it takes to become a success. A funny thing happens when you do this. Not only will you benefit from your hard work, but you never know if someone who is watching can give you the helping hand that you need to catapult you into success.

Obviously, I do not believe that cleaning that bathroom got me to where I am today, but the mindset of being willing to do what others are not has had everything to do with my success. If you want to achieve great successes in your lifetime and create a legacy, adopt the traits in this chapter, as so many successful people before you have. To repeat, they are:

1. Practice action
2. Know how to communicate
3. Know your strengths and weaknesses (and be honest with yourself)
4. Never stop learning
5. Live a healthy lifestyle
6. Practice philanthropy and don't forget where you came from
7. Be competitive
8. Love what you do
9. Become an overcomer
10. Do what others will not do

Chapter 9

Starting a Business... What Does It Take?

The main theme in this book is not just how to become successful and build your business, but how to do it *quickly*. Most of the material has to do with you, the individual, and how you have to think and act to become successful. In the next two chapters, I am going to switch gears and talk more about the tactical side of success. My overall goal is not only to empower you with the mindset you need to become successful, but also to empower you with the knowledge of how to do the simple things, too. These two chapters will give you some details about what it takes to run your own business and will set out the steps you need to take to start a legitimate company recognized by both state and federal governments. I will also cover the idea of developing reliable multiple streams of income, so you can learn how to get out of the constant grind of earning a living and can begin to know what success feels like. Many of the tactics I will talk about are a large part of my success today. It is as important to have the right mindset and systems as it is to know the tactical steps to take to get on the road to success.

Throughout my travels and meetings with people in one form or another, one of the questions that seems to come up more than any other is how to start a business. You may have a great idea or see a great need in your local community, but you don't even know where to start. I can remember the first company I ever formed. I was not only unaware of where to start, but also where to end. Once I started the process, I was always wondering if I had missed something that was going to catch up with me later. I was also unaware of what it took emotionally and personally. Starting a business can drain you more than anything else, if you let it. You will always be thinking of ways to do things better, and you will always have new ideas that you want to implement, especially when it is your own business and you are the sole beneficiary of its success. Unfortunately, you carry the weight of any failure squarely on your own shoulders, as well. You cannot let this happen. You must run your business or it will run you.

This chapter has two parts. The first part is not as tangible as the second, because it talks about what it takes to run a successful business. I don't mean systems or marketing or other operations, but the personal factors that can have a huge effect on your success.

The second part covers the practical steps you need to take to start a business, from creating a business plan to filing certain documents with the state. One of the first steps is deciding what type of business you will be. Will you consider yourself a sole proprietor or a limited liability company? What is the difference? This is the type of decision I hope to clarify for you.

You must understand that many states have different requirements. Although I will give you guidelines, it is wise to check in with your Secretary of the State and find out what steps and documents are required in your state. It is also wise to consult with an attorney when discussing these matters. Many small businesses don't benefit from the advice of a good attorney because they believe that it will cost them too much money. I must say as emphatically as I can: You cannot afford to set up your business incorrectly. I will discuss why in the coming pages.

I will also discuss topics such as partnering and raising capital for your business. Should you consider either of these? Are they necessary? Every business is different and every business model is different. You are doing your job by learning about these topics and you must decide for yourself what will be best for your business.

In short, this chapter is for people who either desire to learn or brush up on the following topics:

What it takes to be in business (successfully)
Do you have 'IT?'
Starting a business
Creating a business plan
Choosing a structure for your business
The steps in creating a business
Should you work with an attorney?
Is partnering a good idea?
Should you raise capital or funding? How do you do it?

What Does It Take to Be in Business?

There is no doubt that certain personalities tend to be more successful in business ventures than others. Usually, this is for obvious reasons. Networking is such a crucial part of your business so it makes sense that someone with natural people skills will have a bit of an edge. Don't underestimate the edge you get just because people like you. This sounds a bit shallow at first – the idea that one person is more successful than another just because people like that person more – but it is true. *The majority of the people who will make your business successful will never know if you are good at what you do until after they have used your services or your company.* Many of your clients will become your clients simply because they like you. This is crucial for you to understand, because it is the difference between building a business that lasts and or watching as your business does nothing but eat away at your savings. After you are hired, these clients will either find out that they like you and you are good at what you do, and they start sending other people to you; or they will like you personally, but come to the conclusion that business is business, and you just don't know what you are doing.

> *The majority of the people who will make your business successful will never know if you are good at what you do until after they have used your services or your company.*

You must work at getting people to like you. For example, if you tend to make dumb comments off the cuff, it is time to make fewer and fewer of these comments. Systems, ideas, and great business models cannot make up for people not liking you. Unfortunately or fortunately, depending on how you look at it, in many ways business is a popularity contest. Consumers 'vote' with their cash for the people they like the most. There are exceptions to this, but not many.

If people do like you, you have only one responsibility: Becoming the best at what you do in your field. When likeability and expertise are combined, the result is dynamite. People love to say, "Use my person" when others are doing something that may require your services. You have probably done this yourself. You find out that someone you know needs a Realtor, contractor, or other supplier, and you make it your personal mission to promote the person you use because you are happy with them. This is why you need the full dynamite effect. If someone just likes you, they will invite you to their next picnic, but they won't promote what you do for a living. If you are just good at what you do, but are not that likeable, your clients are not going to feel comfortable promoting you, because how you interact with others reflects back on them. No one wants to send their friends and family to someone with the personality of a rock, no matter how good you are at your job.

In addition to being likeable and good at what you do, you have to possess inner strength and drive. I like to picture it as having a lion inside of me. Or better, you are a lion with a human costume that you take off at night and put back on in the morning. Unfortunately, if you reach a certain level, some people will test you and try to bring you down. You should have a smile on your face 90% of the time, but whenever needed, learn to call on your inner lion and show your teeth. I have found that diplomacy works with most of the people I meet. It is the other 10% of people that need to have the tone set early on. These people may try to take advantage of you and try to talk down to you. They are really testing you to see if you belong in the big leagues or not. Before you fight back, you had better know the answer to that question yourself. Do you possess an inner lion, or are you still Simba from the Lion King, trying with all of your might to growl but you're not quite there yet?

You will need your inner lion at your loneliest moments, too. Almost all the business owners I know have asked themselves whether they are doing the right thing. Running a business is tough and challenging. There is no boss to complain about when things are not going well. You cannot count on receiving a paycheck every Friday, whether you did well or not that particular week. You succeed or fail because of what YOU do and how YOU do it. It is constant work to find new business and figure out better ways to provide services to your clients. You are always trying to think of new ways to generate income and provide for those you love the most. And yet, if you are doing what you love, you will always come to the same conclusion: That you wouldn't have it any other way.

Early on in my real estate career, I never questioned whether I should be doing what I was doing. But I certainly questioned why I was doing it. I would think about the jobs I could have had at various corporations, the positions I could have held, or the security I could have enjoyed with a weekly paycheck. I remember one particular time when I had a closing set up towards the end of a month. Because some bills were due, this check was spent before I even got it. I hadn't had a closing in a couple of months, so I really needed and was anticipating this check. I think you know where I am going. Lo and behold, one week before the closing, the deal fell apart and I was hit with the harsh reality that I didn't have any income and the bills still needed to get paid. It was crunch time. Did I swallow my pride, tell everyone I made a mistake, and go out to get a good-paying job? Don't think I didn't consider this option more than a little bit. In the end, I still knew in my core what I was supposed to be doing. If you don't know in your core what you should be doing, don't waste your time. If you are constantly allowing external circumstances to change your vision, you probably should not have been doing whatever it was from the beginning. Your purpose on this earth is much stronger than the momentary bind you find yourself in. I like what people used to say to me when I was a child: "Jared, this too shall pass. This too shall pass." Boy, were they telling the truth! You need to adopt this kind of attitude if you are going to succeed.

Do You Have IT?

In sports, you may have heard an announcer or a scout say, "He's got IT" or "She's got IT." Business is no different. Some people have got IT and some people don't. IT is not one particular thing, which is why many different types of people can be successful, but realizing whether you have some form of IT will save you a lot of time and money.

In life, you need to either have IT or follow someone who does, until you obtain your own IT. If you are honest with yourself, you will know which it is. If you don't have IT now, start hanging around with those that do, and IT will start to rub off on you. As the saying goes, "If you want to know who someone is, find out who they hang out with." This is true on many different levels, not only because you tend to hang out with like-minded people, but also because you tend to become more like the people you spend the most time with.

I was fortunate enough to have picked up on this principal at an early age. I have always been drawn to people who seemed to be dynamic and charismatic, mainly because I wanted to get a little bit of what they had. This principal works in the opposite direction, as well. If you hang out with depressed or low-energy people, you will likely notice that you become that way, too. If you don't think you are a high-energy person, think of something you are passionate about, and you will be amazed at how much energy you have for it.

Starting a Business

The first step in starting a business is knowing what you want to do. You may have to try a few different fields before you really figure out what you want to do. Many people would disagree with what I just said. They believe that if you are truly passionate about something, you should already know what you want to do. This sounds great in theory, but many times you can be caught up in the idea of something, and until you actually get out there and do it, you just don't know what it takes. For example, you may love the idea of becoming a professional speaker and talking to large crowds, but if you are afraid to fly, can't stand hotels, and don't like to network, you may be pursuing the wrong career.

Another important factor is what it will cost to start the business. Some businesses require very little spending on overhead, but require 'sweat equity.' Other businesses may require expensive equipment or worksites. If you are not factoring your finances into your decision, you are making a mistake.

You have to look at everything involved when starting a business, not just the glory moments, but also the hard work, problems, and anxieties. We all have a tendency, myself included, of picturing only the bright spots in our new adventure. We picture ourselves standing at the top of the mountain with our hands in the air in triumph, but we forget about the exhausting, life-threatening, ten-hour climb to get there. We picture ourselves in Michael Jordan's shoes hitting the game-winning shot in the NBA Finals, but not the countless hours in the gym running sprints or climbing stairs. If you want to reduce your faulty thinking as much as possible when deciding what kind of business to start, focus on the ugly side of that business and see if you still have a passion for it.

Creating a Business Plan

If you find that you already have or can obtain the majority of what I just wrote about, you are ready to start the process of putting your new business together. The first step is creating a business plan.

A well-written business plan simply lays out your business's strategic objectives and how you will accomplish them. You can use a well-written business plan to communicate these objectives to your staff one day. It will play a key role in the success of your business for many reasons. First and foremost, it serves as a reference point if you get off track and forget what your company is supposed to

> *It is easy to go after every opportunity that comes your way, but the truly successful business owners know what they do best.*

be doing. It is easy to go after every opportunity that comes your way, but the truly successful business owners know what they do best. You are better off being great at fewer things than being good at all things. Second, you need a good business plan if you want to get any sort of financing or loans.

A business plan can be short or as long as 40 pages. There is really no reason to go beyond 40 pages. If you are attempting to get friends and relatives to back your new venture, it should be around four-to-six pages long. If you are attempting to contact banks, venture capitalists, private investors, or entities outside of your immediate circle, you will need to have a more formal business plan that can require the 40 pages.

A good business plan consists of the following:

- **Executive Summary**: This is a one-to-three page explanation of your business and what your business does. Your executive summary should include your primary goals and objectives.

- **Business Description:** This is where you set out your perception of your company. You must describe how you intend to grow and how you will make a profit.

- **The Market and Competition:** This should be one of the longest sections. It is where you give an honest and unbiased assessment of your competition and discuss how you intend to break into their market.

- **The Product or Service**: This is where you describe in detail what you are offering. If it is a product, explain what it is. If it is a service, explain what you do.

- **Selling:** This is where you explain how you will make a splash in the marketplace. Give details about the type of marketing you will do. Will you have a website? What type of networking will you do? The more details you can provide, the better.

- **Management and Personnel:** This is where you set out your management philosophy and explain how you will manage your business. It is wise to include the names of all of your key employees and their biographies, making sure they all look competent, educated, and strong. You do not want them to look as if they could not get a real job, so they decided to give your business a shot.
- **Financial Data:** This section contains your balance sheet, profit-and-loss statement, break-even chart, and cash-flow analysis. If you have not started your business yet, you should create *pro forma* versions of these documents.
- **Investment:** In this section, you describe, based on a realistic cash flow, what kind of return your potential investor can expect.
- **Appendices:** You can include many types of appendices – testimonials from customers, research clips, various relevant charts and graphs, and so forth. The purposes of these appendices are to give potential investors a fuller sense of your business and to demonstrate your knowledge and expertise.

Before starting to write your business plan, decide what type of plan is needed. Are you attempting to get funds from your family, or are you planning to approach banks or similar entities? Do you need outside money at all? Your decision will determine the size and formality of your business plan. I do suggest, though, even if you are planning on approaching only close family members for capital, you should still make your plan as formal and as impressive as possible. For them, $10,000 may be more of a risk than $1,000,000 to the bank.

If you need any further assistance with writing your business plan, I suggest finding a nonprofit organization, such as SCORE ("Counselors to America's Small Business"), to help you. Their website is www.score.org.

Choosing a Structure for Your Business

There are many different types of formal business structures, but four of them, in my opinion, are most appropriate for a new business:

Sole Proprietorships
Partnerships
Corporations
Limited Liability Companies (LLCs)

Sole proprietorships make up over 75% of the small businesses in America, according to the U.S. Small Business Administration. This is probably because this structure is the least expensive and simplest to form. This structure allows you to file your personal and business taxes together on the same return. I am not a huge proponent of this structure, primarily because it leaves you open to legal liability.

Partnerships are businesses with more than one owner. A partnership allows you to divide profits and losses among the partners and are most common among attorneys, doctors, or other professional service providers who share a roof, but bring in their own clients.

Corporations are much more expensive to create, but this form does provide protections for your personal assets if you are sued or your business fails. The corporate form is not typically used by start-up businesses. There are two forms of corporations: S Corporations and C Corporations. S Corporations are sometimes used for small businesses. Under this form, you are not personally liable, and the chance of double taxation is eliminated. But there are limits to your retirement benefits and restrictions on the number of shareholders you can have (no more than 100), and you may have to pay taxes on your benefits. C Corporations also limit your personal liability, give you access to capital through stock sales, and even allows you to transfer ownership. Unfortunately, C Corporations also allow for double taxation and can be costly to start up.

The structure I really want to focus on is a Limited Liability Company (LLC), because this structure works so well for small business owners. An LLC is a state-chartered organization that allows for the reduced personal liability of a corporation, but with the tax advantages of a partnership. Basically, it is the best of both worlds. There are no restrictions on the members involved in your business; there is no double taxation; and it is comparatively easy to raise capital.

All of the businesses I have ever started have been LLCs because I believe that this form gives me the most freedom and is the easiest to start up with the least amount of risk. The last thing you want to do is leave yourself open to risk if you make a mistake in your business.

It is really important to consult an attorney when deciding which is the best option for you. I don't pretend to be an attorney and don't want you to think that reading this chapter is a substitute for legal advice. Ultimately, you should take the time to do the research necessary in your state or country and work with your attorney to determine what is best for you.

Steps for Creating Your Business

Step 1: Reserve the Name. If you are thinking about starting a business and have a name that you love but are not ready to file as a business yet, you should really consider filing to reserve the name with your Secretary of the State. This will let you see whether the name you want is available and, if it is, hold it. In my state, it costs $25 to reserve a name. In many states you can actually check online to see if the name you want is available.

Step 2: File with the Secretary of the State. In most states, you have to file your *articles of organization* so your state knows what you do and that you exist. Contact the office of your Secretary of the State for details. In my state, it costs $60 to file your articles of organization.

Step 3: Complete an Operating Agreement. You should be putting together your operating agreement at the same time you are sending your articles of organization to the Secretary of the State. Your operating agreement names the members of the company and the percentage of the company each member owns. It will also detail, among other things, what kind of equity each member owns, what type of business your company does, and how decisions are made in the company. This is an important document, especially if discrepancies arise.

Step 4: File for your Employee Identification Number (EIN). You can file for your EIN by going to www.IRS.gov. Your EIN is for tax purposes and allows you to open up bank accounts and convey property in your company name. If you buy a property in your company name, instead of using your personal social security number, you now use your company's EIN.

Do You Need an Attorney? This is a good question and an easy one to answer. As I mentioned earlier, I highly recommend getting the advice of an attorney. Consider this: One of the main reasons business owners use the LLC or similar form is for the personal protection it provides them. But, as with anything else, whenever you have something good like this, there will always be those who try to take advantage of it. This has lead to a legal term known as 'piercing the corporate veil.'

Basically, what this means is that if you do not set up your business properly, the very thing that an LLC is supposed to do for you – protect you personally – may leave your personal assets exposed. Because too many people were setting up LLCs for themselves solely to protect their assets, without actually acting like an LLC, the courts have found that you must prove that you are an actual LLC and are not just taking advantage of the system. One mistake in how you set up your business structure could lead to everything you have worked for your whole life being at risk. There is no doubt in my mind that it is worth the extra step of consulting an attorney when making such an important move.

Is Partnering a Good Idea? Partnering for the right reasons can be a very good idea. Too often I see people become partners because they are friends, but this is not a good reason to be partners. In fact, this may be even more of a reason not to be partners. Why take a chance of ruining a beautiful friendship if you don't have to?

The question I suggest people ask themselves when considering a partner is, "Do you need them?" It is really that simple. If they don't bring some asset or skill that you don't already have or could easily acquire, what is the point of partnering? If you think it would be great to have a partner to share the workload, then just hire someone as a part of the staff or as a manager. Don't bring someone on as a partner.

Questions to ask about potential partners are: Do they offer capital that you need? Do they offer expertise that you need? Do they have significant contacts that you will need? Additionally, you and your potential partners are going to need to discuss certain matters up front, such as:

Who makes the decisions? If there are two of you and you don't agree, who makes the decision? I recommend making sure that your operating agreement lists one partner as the 51% owner and the other as the 49% owner, so one of you can make a decision in the event of a disagreement.

How is equity split? Is it determined by the percentage of capital that each partner put in at the beginning? Usually, it is easier to determine the equity split by making it equivalent to the percentage of the initial capital that each partner provided. Sometimes, you have to take into account factors such as sweat equity though, where one partner earns their percentage of equity through hard work. Either way, your equity agreement needs to be in writing. Remember that all of your agreements must be in writing no matter how close you are to your partners.

How will you handle succession plans? What happens if one partner wants to leave the business? Can that one partner decide who will take over his or her shares, even if the other partner doesn't agree? This is important because that original partner went into partnership with a particular person, not that person's friend or child whom they don't even know.

What are your roles? Roles have to be determined and defined from the beginning. Does one person handle personnel and the other handles the finances? These decisions have to be made up front or problems will tear your business apart.

Should You Raise Capital or Funding? How Do You Do It?
Whether you raise capital or funding for your new business is really a personal question determined by your individual circumstances. If you do need to raise money for your new venture, the lender is going to want to know the answers to three questions:

What do you need money for?
How long will you need it?
How are you going to pay me back?

If you don't have answers to these three simple questions, no one will lend you money, not even your own mother. Part of being able to answer these questions is having a good business plan that details what your company does and how it is going to take advantage of certain market conditions to make money to pay your investors back.

It is important to understand that there are short-term and long-term ways to raise capital. I would never recommend taking out a short-term loan to pay for a long-term need. A general rule is to match the term of the loan to both the length of the need and to the source of repayment. Using a 90-day note for permanent financing needs is very risky and not necessary. If you do this, you are risking that the loan will not be renewed, but additionally, you are putting yourself in a position where you can never plan more than 90 days ahead.

There are many different avenues you could explore for initial capital for your business, including:

Business credit cards
Business credit lines
Short-term loans
Home equity lines of credit
Profit-sharing funds from your previous job
Friends and family
Local and national banks
Venture capitalists
Personal savings
Personal credit cards

There are many others sources of capital, some more risky than others. I really do not suggest going too far into debt to start a business, especially credit card debt with high interest rates where compound interest starts to work against you.

It is important for you to understand that other factors outside of your business plan influence whether someone will lend you money as well. One is your personal credit score, and another is the type of collateral you use to back your loan.

Your personal credit score tells a person or institution whether you pay your bills on time. If your credit score is not at least in the high 600s, you may need to take some time to build it before you approach others about lending to you.

The collateral could be equity in your house, a car you have paid off, or some other tangible item of value. People looking to lend you a significant amount of money will want to know that their loan is secured by something. Most banks won't even consider you without some form of collateral.

In an ideal world you would not have to look to others for financing. I have always been a proponent of doing everything from a position of strength. As much as possible, don't trap yourself by becoming indebted to more people than you have to. If that means that you take longer to achieve your dream, then take your time. It is not enough that you are going after what you think you are supposed to be doing with your life. If you go too fast or try to do something at the wrong time, you can do more damage than is necessary. There is a time for everything. If you hold on to this mindset you will be more cautious about going into debt, even when it is necessary.

About six months ago, I was coaching a real estate agent on how to succeed in a down market. I went over my business strategies, marketing plans, and systems, just to give this Realtor an idea of what has to be done to succeed, while almost everyone else seems to be drowning. This agent thought about everything I had shown him and came back to me the next day with an idea. He was

If a business grows at the speed of light overnight, it can come crashing down in a day's time, as well.

going to get a business credit card and write a check off of it into his own bank account so he would have the money to do the same kind of marketing that I currently do. A stop sign should have just popped up in your head. This is a terrible idea. There is nothing wrong with growing your business at a slower pace for sustained growth. Take it a little at a time. If a business grows at the speed of light overnight, it can come crashing down in a day's time, as well. On the other hand, if your business grows over time and establishes a solid foundation, it is much more likely to persevere through the tough times. Especially if you don't have large debt payments due every month to cover the loan you incurred to start the business.

If you do raise capital for your business, just make sure that you need to do so and you will be able to pay the debt back in a timely manner. When it is used appropriately, a loan can be a very positive thing for your company and can be a catapult for growth that you never could have reached without a needed infusion of capital.

Chapter 10

Developing Multiple Streams of Income

I have been developing multiple streams of income my whole life, whether consciously or subconsciously. Very simply, this means that I have developed ways to have income streaming in from various sources, so I am not relying on my job or business as my only income producer.

Think about it: This is what the world's largest companies do on a grand scale. AT&T didn't start out by servicing phones, supporting Blackberries, and providing Internet service. GE didn't begin by having its hands in appliances, aviation, energy, finance, lighting, health care, oil and gas, and media and entertainment. Both companies expanded their scope of business to include additional fields over time.

You can do the same thing on a smaller scale. To do so, you need vision and the ability to look beyond where you are and see the possibilities for where you want to go. You have to be able to see the big picture and understand what your goals are and what you want for you and your family. Once you identify those goals, you need to take some time and brainstorm what you are good at. Here are some questions to ask yourself when brainstorming:

Question 1: What do I enjoy doing? What are my hobbies? Many people don't realize that they can make money doing what they love. Think about friends or acquaintances who have started photography and film businesses on the side or have even made money booking gigs for their bands. Some people are paid to shop and give their opinions. Yes, you heard that right – some people are paid to shop and give opinions on the products. What could be better than doing something you would do anyway, but getting a paycheck for it?

Question 2: What unique skills do I possess? You have to figure out what you do better than the majority of the population. Everyone is good at something, even if they don't realize it yet. You, along with a lot of others, may be good at a broad skill, so you might not realize that the skill is worthwhile. But figure out what subcategory of the skill you like most and are best at and you might find that there is a great demand for it. For example, a lot of people may have the skill to bake cakes, but your unique skill is baking *multi-layer* cakes. It is much easier to market this unique skill because your competition can't provide the same products. You are developing a special niche. Spend some time figuring out what your special niche is.

Question 3: What need could I meet in my location or even online? I like to tell people to try to find a need and then fill it, preferably in a field that has the least amount of competition. Remember, your other streams of income will be in addition to your current work so it doesn't make sense to pick something that is going to take five years of nights and weekends to develop. That would go against one of my strongest principles, which is to put your family first and make sure that you are spending QUALITY time with them. Keeping this principle in mind is crucial when deciding how you are going to make extra income. The best way to identify needs in your area is to think about products or services that you wish were available to you. My wife and I often find ourselves wanting certain children's products. When we started feeding my first son, we put a bib on him, which protected him from getting food on himself, but the cleanup needed on the floor afterwards was unbelievable. Now, our second son is wearing a new bib that has a catcher on the bottom to keep food from falling to the floor. My instinct is to say, "Why didn't I think of that?" That is your job now: To start to think like that.

With the almost-daily changes in technologies and ways of doing business, there are constantly new ways to improve consumers' experiences and make their lives easier. Just as in the past where someone took a nail file and made millions calling it an envelope opener, there are plenty of opportunities for you to find now. Today's consumer is health conscious, but rushed; maybe there should be a drive-through at every Subway sandwich shop. Or, many people who have been laid off have always wanted to start their own businesses and will decide that now is their time to do it. And new start-ups need graphic designers who can create logos and other branding materials. So if you have graphic design skills, why not start a Graphic Design Studio out of your own house? The possibilities are endless.

The growth of the Internet has made it much easier to have another income stream. You don't even need to see or talk to your customers anymore. You can charge their credit cards and get shipping information and feedback from them, without ever knowing if they are male or female. This has made it very possible to grow a products-based business from your own home if you have the right product and an effective website.

Question 4: What contacts do I have in similar fields that could help me? One of your goals is to figure out how to break into an additional field with the greatest amount of ease. Why swim up a stream if you are being offered a boat with a motor? You may know people who have contacts that can help you get your new business off the ground a whole lot faster. A great example of this would be if you decided to develop your additional stream of income by making customized tee shirts and uniforms and found out that a business acquaintance knows the head of marketing at a major corporation that is changing its uniforms and is looking for bids. Obviously, it would be a huge boost to your income and your credibility to get this work because you could now list this major company as a client of yours. This example shows how one contact can change the face of your business, while a competitor is making cold calls, one business at a time, hoping to sell ten or fifteen tee shirts to make a few extra dollars. Do you see the difference contacts can make? Many times you have such contacts but you are not asking the right questions or thinking in the right frame of mind to even notice them when they are right in front of you. Use your contacts to the fullest. If you don't, someone else will. Often business success really is more about who you know than what you know. Once you get your foot in the door, you can show that you deserve the opportunity they are giving you by offering them great customer service and having a product that speaks for itself.

Question 5: How much will it cost to get started? This is a big question, which many people are afraid to ask because the answer may be what they think it is. Ignorance is bliss, and it would be nice if we could ignore the realities. If at all possible, try to develop a business that doesn't require you to spend a lot of money until you have sales or clients. Most likely, though, you are going to have to spend some kind of money up front if you want to portray yourself as credible. (I will talk about my experiences below.) You will probably need to develop a logo and a website, and you will need stationery and business cards. Depending on your type of business, you may be able to find a company that supplies templates so you don't have to pay thousands of dollars to a web designer at first, although eventually you'll find that good web designers can be worth their weight in gold. A local graphic designer, or even an online designer, can develop your logo and stationery for a few hundred dollars or so, depending on your requirements. Printing costs depend on the quantities you need. I recommend getting about 500-1000 business cards printed for around $50-$100, and a few hundred sheets of letterhead and envelopes for around $200. You could even save money by running blank envelopes through your printer and printing your company information on them yourself. You can save money on envelopes without jeopardizing your credibility, but I do not recommend trying to save money on business cards.

How much you have to invest up front depends on your situation and the field you are entering. Regardless, you should try to keep these costs as low as possible until you have established your cash flow. The lesson to learn here is to minimize your exposure to risk as much as possible without shutting the door on possible reward. Success is in the balance.

Making Synergy Work for You

Ideally, you will be able to find something in a field that parallels what you currently do so you can work on both businesses in the same day and use the contacts you have already made. This is important, because it allows you to work smart, while working hard. Some people have taken the concept of developing multiple streams of income and have gone out and worked a full-time job, sold cosmetics on the side, and built a landscaping business on the weekends. Although they have multiple streams of income, they are breaking their backs and don't have time to enjoy the fruits of their labor. That is not at all what I am talking about.

When I first started in real estate I had a pretty simple business model: I helped people buy and sell houses. It didn't matter if it was a single family house, condo, co-op, or multi-family house. My job was to sell houses. As my career began to progress, I saw more and more opportunities coming my way. I can remember the first time a man called me and asked if I handled commercial real estate. I hadn't sold a commercial property in my life and didn't know how to do much more than turn the lights on and off in an office building. But do you know what my response was? "Of course I sell commercial real estate. I would be an idiot for not covering such a large area of the real estate market if I didn't handle commercial real estate as well." Immediately following this conversation where I won an Academy Award for answering his questions well and dodging the ones I couldn't answer at the time, I hunted for everything anyone could need to know about commercial real estate. I have always believed that the best way to learn is by doing. Here was my chance to prove it.

I called everyone I knew who did commercial real estate, I searched the Internet for every bit of information I could find, and I got an answer for every possible question this man could ask me. Additionally, I redesigned my website to include a commercial section and added an article "10 Questions to Ask when Purchasing a Commercial Property" by Jared James. This is how you have to think to be successful. By the time I met this man face-to-face to talk with him about purchasing a commercial property, I was an expert, because I had studied as if my life depended on it. More importantly, I was expanding my business to include a new field and thereby creating another source of income. In the end, I made over $50,000 from this client over the next three months. If I had narrowed my mind to cover only what I was currently doing, can you imagine how disappointed I would have been watching someone else collect that commission?

A little while later, I was asked by a technology company to try their database system for free. I did try it and actually liked it a lot. The owner of the company then told me about an opportunity he was offering to real estate agents who liked the product. He would send me a list of other realtors in my region who wanted to try the product. These were 'hot leads:' They already knew about the product and wanted more information; they were ready to buy and wanted someone to contact them. The opportunity involved me spending time calling these other realtors and telling them that I loved the product. In return, when these other agents signed up, I would receive a cut of their fees every month that they continued to use the product.

It made a lot of sense to me. On average, I would get about $5 per agent per day, and my closing rate was around 90%. Mathematically, if I made 10 calls a day and signed up 9 people, I would build a residual income of $45 a day (9 people times $5 per person), or about $225 a week, and the amount would grow week-by-week and month-by-month. Before long, I would have a whole other stream of income coming in that would cover all of my bills for less than an hour's work. I couldn't lose, right?

Well, the math made sense and the business model was great, but I never saw even one paycheck from that company. It turned out that there were legal issues between the two partners in the company; one sued the other right after their initial launch and the company shut down. I wasted a lot of time that I could have used to do more productive tasks. Why am I telling you about this failure? Because you learn something from everything you do and everyone you meet. In this case, I could have been completely turned off and could have made up my mind to avoid all of these additional income 'gimmicks.' Or, I could open up my mind to recognize that, although this particular gimmick burned me, the idea of doing something that I was talented at in a limited amount of time and getting paid big time for it was a good one. I remembered this lesson when the next opportunity presented itself.

In 2007, the real estate market was definitely on a decline. Bankruptcies and foreclosures were reaching all-time highs. As any good business professional would do, I decided to focus on the opportunities that the market presented instead of dwelling on the dismal statistics being reported daily by the media. It was amazing. If the housing market decreased by 1.8%, the media called it Armageddon.

Regardless, I knew that, given the number of foreclosures and pre-foreclosures, a lot of investors would be licking their chops and trying to get at these bargains. While many buyers were running scared, successful investors thought like me and saw opportunity. By this time, I had established myself enough in my local market so people were bringing me deals to see if I had buyers for them. Many times I did and I made a lot of money for investors. I found the deals for them, told them what it would cost to do the deal, let them know what they could sell them for, and negotiated their contracts. There were so many deals that everyone benefited. You could be picky because better deals came along everyday. I was really getting tired of making so much money for everyone else, though. Yes, I profited on the deals through commissions, but I was making nowhere near what the investors were making.

Near the end of 2007, someone told me he had just received a bonus and he really thought now would be a great time to get into the market but he just didn't have the time. Ding, ding, ding. Bells went off in my head. This could be the perfect partnership and opportunity for both of us. He had the money and I had the expertise and time. We talked a little more and decided to launch a real estate investment company aimed at capitalizing on the current market conditions and the apprehensions of other buyers. We weren't afraid to buy, as long as it was at the right price.

At the beginning of 2008, we bought our first investment property. It was a mess. There was a blue tarp over the roof to minimize the leaking, a broken-down car in the yard, and old expired food mashed into the floors all over the house. I was able to use the contacts I had already made from my real estate business to clean up, list, and sell the property. We had the satisfaction of not only making money, but also having the neighbors come up to us at our Open House to tell us how much they appreciated what we did with this eyesore in their neighborhood. It was a win for everyone. I even made a commission on the original purchase.

We went on to purchase more houses that year at deeply-discounted prices due to market conditions and frequently the seller's particular circumstances. Some sellers were trying to avoid foreclosure, so a quick sale would benefit them more than a high price. One couple wanted to move down south to be closer to their children, but they needed to be out by a certain date and they didn't want to have to worry about how long their house would be on the market or whether it would sell at all. They too gave us a steep discount. The key for us was to find out the seller's motivation. Our niche was sellers who were not motivated by price. We were able to buy these particular houses and resell them quickly at just below current market value before we ever had to make a single mortgage payment or do any renovations. And we did it all for a profit.

The beauty of it all was that this other stream of income was just a natural extension of what I was already doing everyday. It was amazing how naturally my investment business fit in with my daily real estate business. Because of the large number of opportunities out there, I could make additional money myself and still satisfy my investment clients. The key was not getting greedy. I never compromised my standing as a real estate agent and made sure that all the sellers l contacted as an investor knew I had my real estate license. I never competed with one of my buyers for a property. This is the biggest mistake I see many investors make: Getting greedy and compromising their values to the point where they start to operate in a gray area.

I wound up making an additional six figures of income that year with my investment company. It became quite a stream of income and still allowed me to be home for dinner every night to spend time with my family. Having that time is the natural by-product of finding a stream of income that naturally meshes with what you already do if at all possible.

Benefits of Multiple Streams of Income

Being home for dinner is only one of the many benefits that having multiple streams of income can bring. My experience has shown me three additional benefits: money, security (through diversity), and contacts.

Money

The obvious result of having income streaming in from more than one place is more money, right? Well, not necessarily. If you work at a job that is commission-based or performance-based and you take on the wrong venture to make more money, you could actually make less money because your primary source of income may suffer. This is why choosing the right venture is so important.

If you make the right decision, you will bring in more money through your various sources of income. Remember the example of my commercial real estate business and my investment business? It is realistic to say that over the last few years the businesses combined have made me hundreds of thousands of dollars. I don't know what that means to you, but when I was growing up people who made six figures in a year were considered rich, even without making an *additional* six figures in a year.

Many people believe that just a little more money will solve all of their problems, but this is simply not true. Usually, the same people who were broke making $30,000 a year, are even more broke when they make $50,000 a year. The key is to budget properly and respect money for what it is worth. If you do this, there is no doubt that having extra cash feels good. It is nice to be able to take your family on a vacation without racking up credit card debt, or to get special toys for your kids because you love them, or to bless your spouse with a piece of jewelry and know that you can afford to own that piece of jewelry outright. There is something to be said for having the mindset of frugality (and trust me, I have it), but still being able to spend money on the things that make sense, such as housing or furniture. It is money well spent to purchase items that can either appreciate in value or last a long time. Many people think they save money by buying

> *If you make the right decision, you will bring in more money through your various sources of income.*

cheap furniture, but these same people have to buy furniture again every few years.

Security/Diversity

When you have more money coming in, it is much easier to feel a sense of security. I grew up worrying frequently about how the bills were going to get paid. I can vividly remember my mother coming home from a job interview crying because the interviewer told her that they couldn't hire her because she was overqualified and they didn't think she would stay at the job. I remember her saying to herself with tears on her face that being overqualified wasn't going to pay the landlord or her bills. I can still picture the stress and anxiety on her face. I felt so helpless as a young child and didn't know what to say or do for her, but I knew I didn't want to be in the same position ever again in my life.

Having multiple streams of income has given me the security to know that I don't have to worry about the bills. I am aware of them, but I don't worry about them. There is a big difference between the two. The majority of Realtors can have great financial success in one month, but worry about their bills the very next month because they don't have any guaranteed income coming in. I have been fortunate enough to be able to pay the bills, put money away for retirement, save for my children's college education, put money in savings, and even invest some in real estate and the stock market. Over time, I have been able to put money in different places and know that my family and I are safe. This may not sound like a big deal, but for someone raised in financial instability as I was, it is extremely important, not just for me personally, but for my children who I know don't have to worry.

Some people have questioned whether I needed the multiple streams of income to become secure because I was doing well at real estate before I branched out. I might have been fine, but for other people, having multiple streams of income may be essential. Some may finally be able to catch up and pay their bills. Others may try to start to save some money. And a few will be able to get ahead and start to plan for the future. You may find yourself in all three situations, but your ultimate goal should be to get ahead and plan for the future.

Just as good financial planners diversify their holdings as they invest in the stock market, having multiple streams of income allows you to diversify. When you are not depending on one income, you don't have to worry as much about the cyclical nature of almost every industry on this planet. As I mentioned above, when real estate in general was down, my real estate investing was up. If I had only relied on one aspect of real estate, I might have been in trouble. When the real estate market turns around, there may not be quite as many foreclosures and opportunities as there are now. Who knows? But it is nice to know that I am diversified enough to be successful no matter what happens in the economy. And I haven't even mentioned my work in the commercial real estate sector, which has remained relatively strong compared to the residential

> *Diversifying allows you to be proactive in managing how the external climate affects you.*

market. This is all part of positioning yourself for success. Diversifying allows you to be proactive in managing how the external climate affects you.

Contacts

The last benefit of having multiple streams of income is the contacts that you make. Think about all the contacts you currently make just working at your one job now. When you are running one, two, or three money-making operations, your contact database doubles, triples, and even quadruples.

A year ago, I was on a cable television show called *Flip This House*. I can't tell you how many calls I got from people who were watching and saw me. Or clients who say, "Weren't you on *Flip This House*?" My appearance on the show came from some contacts I had made from my investment company. I would never have gotten this exposure if it hadn't been for an income stream outside of my main career.

Every time you do business, you are making contact with other people. Do not overlook this. Too many people are so focused on the result of a transaction that they don't focus on the people involved. For the most part, the product you are selling cannot refer you to another client or introduce you to someone who can further your career. It is wise to remember that you never know who you are talking to. I have been amazed at some of the people I've met along my path who have helped me, especially the ones I never expected to help. I pride myself on being able to size someone up very quickly and on having an ability to gauge what my relationship with this person should be. Even so, I am very deliberate in my interactions with just about every person I do business with.

You never want to burn a bridge and you never know who you are making an impression on.

A Final Thought

The idea of multiple streams of income can be hard to grasp when you are struggling to keep even one income coming in, but I want you to expand your mind. Sometimes you will fail and sometimes other people will fail you, as when the company I was making sales for closed down. But that doesn't mean you should give up. I am convinced that most people give up right before they make it. You have to picture yourself in a Rocky movie, where no matter how many times you get knocked down, you get back up. But there comes a time when you should aspire to put the 'underdog' behind you. Underdogs are underdogs because they have a history of losing or are overmatched and expected to lose. It may be all right to be the underdog for a short period of time, but your mindset should always be one that looks forward and says, "It's winning time!"

Afterword

Jared James is the CEO and Founder of Jared James Enterprises LLC. His company was formed to teach and coach Realtors on how to drastically increase their sales volume in a short amount of time, along with a selection of other pertinent topics. He travels all over the United States, speaking to and working with Realtors through courses, conferences, webinars, and face-to-face meetings. One of the main themes he develops at all of his meetings and conferences is the idea of having balance in your life. If you would like to contact Jared or book Jared as a speaker for an upcoming event, go to www.jaredjamestoday.com for all the information you will need.

If you are a Realtor and are interested in one of Jared's courses designed to help you make more money and have more time for yourself, visit www.jaredjamestoday.com for a full list of products and courses available. You can email Jared James Enterprises at info@jaredjamestoday.com.

Part of Jared's ongoing work is providing regularly scheduled webinars and conferences for Realtors. If you would like to get more information about upcoming events or register for an upcoming event, you can do so by going to www.jaredjamestoday.com.

Bibliography

I consider the following books good reading for people interested in becoming successful.

Paul Addison, *Churchill: The Unexpected Hero*
Jane Atkinson, *The Wealthy Speaker*
Donny Deutsch, *Often Wrong, Never in Doubt*
Tony Dungy, *Quiet Strength*
Rudy Giuliani, *Leadership*
Billy Graham, *Just As I Am: The Autobiography of Billy Graham*
Bill O'Reilly, *Who's Looking Out for You?*
Tim Russert, *Big Russ and Me*
Donald Trump, *The Art of the Comeback*
Donald Trump, *The Art of the Deal*
Donald Trump, *Think Like a Billionaire*
Ted Turner, *Call Me Ted*
Reggie White, *God's Playbook*

Index

About the Author

Jared James was raised in humble circumstances, which taught him the value of hard work. As he got older and gained more experiences, he intuitively began to pick up on more and more principles of success and began to apply them. These principles, when combined with his blue-collar upbringing, have proven to be the perfect match.

After leaving a successful career to pursue his passion in real estate, it didn't take long for Jared to make a name for himself. In his first year as a Realtor he won "rookie of the year". The following year he decided to start a team and within two years was one of the top 2 teams in the State of Connecticut.

When the economy took a downturn and the real estate market seemed doomed, Jared decided to see opportunity over negativity and saw his business income increase by over 70% while the overall market around him was declining by over 30%.

One of Jared passions has always been to not only succeed, but to help others experience success as well. As a result, he has traveled around the country speaking to and coaching other Realtors on how to drastically improve their sales volume in a short amount of time, just as he did.

It is because of this that Jared was named by Realtor Magazine as one of their "30 under 30" in America.

None of this means anything to him without having a great family to enjoy it all with. Jared has a beautiful and loving wife and two boys that inspire him to keep growing and striving for more.

Breinigsville, PA USA
19 October 2009
226068BV00004B/80/P

9 781601 458551